'he date shown be'
may be renewe
'ote the nu
This ca

D1587010

This book encapsulates Patrick's many years of experience in his gardening practice. His accessible writing style and practical to benefit from his experience, whilst being encouraged to experiment for themselves, to create their own unique relationship with their garden so that it can nourish them in every way.

Caroline Aitken

permaculture teacher, author and director of Patrick Whitefield Associates

This collection of Patrick's writings show what a clear-thinking and knowledgeable pioneer he was. Shining through with tremendous value is his obvious practical experience.

Martin Crawford

author of *Creating A Forest Garden* and *Trees for Gardens, Orchards and Permaculture*

This book is an accessible and easy to read introduction to gardening as an expression of permaculture design. With the chatty style when sharing personal experience, this is Patrick at his best. Well illustrated and laid out (in the excellent style we have come to expect of this publisher) it will be a welcome addition to the fans of Patrick's work, who have enjoyed his detailed observation and analysis in his 'notebook style' over the years.

Graham Bell

permaculture teacher and author of *The Permaculture Way* and *The Permaculture Garden*

Minimalist gardening acts as a gentle 'gateway portal' into the wider realm of regenerative design, one of the most positive and empowering things we can do to help the planet and each other. This book is a fitting tribute to a very special man.

Graham Burnett

author of *Permaculture: A Beginner's Guide* and *The Vegan Book of Permaculture*

Full of practical, achievable real life examples and projects this book is a wonderfully comprehensive guide to growing a productive, low maintenance garden in a small space. A great collection of Patrick's lifetime of permaculture knowledge and wisdom.

Anni Kelsey

author of *Edible Perennial Gardening*

This book carries on and strengthens the legacy that Patrick has left to humanity, stronger for those fortunate to have known him. Its effectiveness will definitely be seen in the number of people able to create, nurture and enjoy diverse, abundant, beautiful and resilient gardens. And he'll look down and be very contented!

Chris Evans

permaculture pioneer, designer and teacher

The Minimalist Gardener is full of sound and sensible information, especially for those setting out to create a garden but also for more established gardeners interested in permaculture. The book introduces permaculture in a gentle way without getting bogged down with principles. It also outlines some of the ways in which wider aspects of permaculture may be adopted to improve our lives and our 'ecological footprint'. *The Minimalist Gardener* is a great legacy of good sense that was a characteristic of Patrick's life and work.

Richard Webb
landscape architect, ecologist and permaculture teacher

I love the clarity of Patrick's language and explanations. His writing is practical and realistic and his sense of humour gently shines through. This book helps both budding and experienced permaculturists to get inspired and get doing.

Klaudia van Gool
permaculture teacher and practitioner

Once again Patrick Whitefield enchants the reader with his calm and warm way of sharing his incredible experience, this time specifically about gardening. The chapters of this book are like taking a walk with Patrick in his garden. Inspiring and practical, a quick guide that will help design even the smallest plot to the readers wants. Permaculture is not about gardening, but gardening is at the heart of permaculture. Patrick Whitefield is always my preferred author.

Lorenzo Costa
permaculture practitioner, DIYer and future farmer in Italy

Patrick guides us to do this in a way that works for any garden size, style or budget, as well as, a particular gardener's time and energy, including how often their garden gets attention. His aim is minimising the work so that gardening is "more like steering a boat than rowing one" which should appeal to people who want to make a difference, but worry they are too busy to garden. Following his advice readers will be able to "put a salad or a pot of greens on the table any day of the year".

Suzie Cahn
permaculture designer and teacher at Carraig Dúlra,
a permaculture education and research farm in Co. Wicklow, Ireland

Packed with design principles and examples for small gardens, Patrick's down-to-earth legacy continues to inspire.

Ben Law
woodsman, ecobuilder and author of *The Woodland Way* and *The Woodland House*

The
Minimalist
Gardener

Brainse Ráth Maonais
Rathmines Branch
Fón / Tel: 4973539

Patrick Whitefield

Permanent Publications

Leabharlanna Poibli Chathair Baile Átha Cliath
Dublin City Public Libraries

Published by
Permanent Publications
Hyden House Ltd
The Sustainability Centre
East Meon
Hampshire GU32 1HR
United Kingdom
Tel: +44 (0)1730 823 311
Fax: +44 (0)1730 823 322
Email: enquiries@permaculture.co.uk
Web: www.permanentpublications.co.uk

Distributed in the USA by
Chelsea Green Publishing Company, PO Box 428, White River Junction, VT 05001
www.chelseagreen.com

© 2017 Patrick Whitefield. The right of Patrick Whitefield to be identified as the author of
this work has been asserted by him in accordance with the Copyrights, Designs and
Patents Act 1988

Designed and typeset by Rozie Apps

Index by Zoe Ross, zoe@sargasso.uk.com

Printed in the UK by Cambrian Printers, Aberystwyth, Wales

All paper from FSC certified mixed sources

The Forest Stewardship Council (FSC) is a non-profit international
organisation established to promote the responsible management of
the world's forests. Products carrying the FSC label are independently
certified to assure consumers that they come from forests that are
managed to meet the social, economic and ecological needs of present
and future generations.

British Library Cataloguing-in-Publication Data
A catalogue record for this book is available from the British Library

ISBN 978 1 85623 285 2

All rights reserved. No part of this publication may be reproduced, stored in a retrieval
system, rebound or transmitted in any form or by any means, electronic, mechanical,
photocopying, recording or otherwise, without the prior permission of Hyden House
Limited.

Contents

About the Author

Patrick Whitefield (11th February 1949 – 27th February 2015) was an early pioneer of permaculture, adapting Bill Mollison's teachings with a strong Southern Hemisphere bias to a cooler, maritime climate such as the British Isles. He wrote a number of seminal books, *Permaculture in a Nutshell* (1993), *How to Make a Forest Garden* (1996), a new edition of *Tipi Living* (2000), *The Living Landscape* (2009), *How To Read the Landscape* (2014) and his magnum opus, *The Earth Care Manual* (2004), an authoritative resource on practical, tested, cool temperate permaculture.

Patrick was born on 11th February 1949 in Devizes, Wiltshire and brought up on a smallholding in Somerset. He qualified in agriculture at Shuttleworth College, Bedfordshire and after several years working in agriculture in the Middle East and Africa, he settled in central Somerset.

Patrick has appeared in several BBC TV programmes, made popular YouTube videos and was a consulting editor of *Permaculture* magazine since its launch in 1992. Patrick taught many permaculture and other practical courses with his wife, Cathy, and was one of the first teachers in the world to develop an online Permaculture Design Course.

After Patrick's death, there were obituaries in *The Telegraph*, *The Guardian* and on BBC Radio 4, and tributes to him from all over the world on social media. Patrick Holden from The Sustainable Food Trust wrote, "It is only towards the end of his life that the wider significance of permaculture ideas began to emerge ... the true significance of Whitefield's ideas was not adequately acknowledged during his lifetime, but his influence will survive him..."

Introduction

We had just published our first book with Patrick, *Permaculture In A Nutshell*, in the early 1990s and were beginning to get to know him and what an extraordinary person he was. We subsequently decided to pay him and his wife, Cathy, a visit in Devon where they were living. They were in a rented house with a small garden and knew they were only there for a short while before moving on. Patrick and Cathy had therefore not invested a great deal of time in their garden. Even so, Patrick took us into the garden to pick a salad to accompany supper. At the time, our eyes were still permaculturally and horticulturally relatively untrained, and we could not see where this salad was going to materialise from. As Patrick explained about wild plants and perennial plants we started to tune in and see that by working with Nature, he and Cathy had created a space that produced a surprising amount of food with hardly any effort. Taken aback by this wild looking small space, Tim said, "This is what I would call a minimalist garden!" Thus the idea of the minimalist garden and Patrick as the minimalist gardener was born.

Patrick had been experimenting with a low maintenance yet productive way of gardening that would feed them for most of the year. The emphasis was on growing perennial and self-seeding edible plants with soft fruit and top fruit where space allowed. His gardens were always managed in as natural a way as possible, using mulch to increase fertility, prevent the growth of weeds and maintain moisture. Using no dig methods, there was not a fork or spade in sight, just a few simple hand tools for planting and weeding. The aim was to minimise the work by only planting favoured annual crops and to grow as many perennials and self-seeders as possible. Nature would share the work.

Of course, there can never be a productive garden that is 100% untended. In *The Minimalist Gardener*, however, Patrick explains that permaculture design will maximise yield and minimise work. One example is the intelligent placement of elements in situations where they will function best (like sun-loving plants in the sunniest place in the garden). He takes us through the design process, mulching, fertility, favoured annuals and perennial vegetables, the placement of plants, easy plants to grow, styles of raised beds, what fruit trees to grow and how to look after them. Gardening was a passion of Patrick's and his pleasure in growing and eating his own food shines out of these pages.

Each of these chapters was first published in *Permaculture* magazine which Patrick wrote for regularly and for which he was a consulting editor from 1992 until he died in 2015. He wrote them because he loved sharing his experience and encouraging everyone to grow even just a little of their own food. He was a dedicated environmentalist with a deep concern for the well-being of our planet. He knew that gardening and growing food for the table does two things. It helps us connect more deeply with natural cycles and seasonal rhythms. This in itself is grounding and helps us to rebalance our stressful lives. He also knew that food contributes up to 30% of our ecological footprint. So much of what we find in the shops is imported, flown thousands of miles to reach our plates, and wrapped in plastic. Growing our own chemical-free food is one of the healthiest things we can do. Patrick was also very practical. He preferred to live simply and he knew that growing food also shrinks the household budget significantly.

Patrick was respected and admired by many. For this reason, we decided to open our archives and bring together this collection of articles into a book, both to celebrate the man and to appreciate his legacy. We hope you find this collection as useful and encouraging as we do.

Maddy and Tim Harland
Editors and co-founders of
Permaculture magazine and Permanent Publications

Monoculture

Both photographs taken from the same position 18 years apart

Permaculture

Patrick Whitefield's garden, three years after implementing the design.

1

Permaculture Gardening

Gardening is at the very heart of permaculture. Our main aim is to reduce our ecological footprint and the biggest single component of our footprint is the food system. Most of this is not due to the actual growing of the food but to the transport, processing and distribution of it. All these ecological costs can be eliminated by growing food in our own home gardens. Even if we only grow some of our own food, it is one of the most effective things we can do to help the planet.

It's also a positive and empowering thing we can do to help the planet. Many of the other ways we can reduce our footprint are a matter of not doing something, like driving a car or flying, or at least cutting down. But gardening is something we can actively do and enjoy.

Two Approaches

Permaculture takes natural ecosystems as its models. There are two ways we can use these models in a garden.

The first is a literal imitation, copying the physical features of natural ecosystems. Its classic expression is in a forest garden, where fruit trees, soft fruit and perennial vegetables are grown together in an imitation of a natural woodland. I call this Original Permaculture because it's how permaculture started out when Bill Mollison and David Holmgren conceived the idea.

The second is what I call Design Permaculture. This flows from an understanding of what makes natural ecosystems work: the network of beneficial relationships between their components, plant, animal and non-living. An example is the relationship between flowering plants and pollinating insects, where one gets its reproductive needs met and the other gets its food. An ecosystem has an uncountable number of relationships like this going on all the time.

We can set up gardens – and other systems – which have this web of relationships without them looking like natural ecosystems at all. The components of the garden can be quite normal and methods apparently conventional, but the positioning of the components is of the essence. That's why design is central to this approach to permaculture.

A simple example is positioning a greenhouse. If it stands alone it loses heat in all directions as soon as the sun goes down. But if it's attached to the south side of a

A raised bed polyculture of beans and sweet corn.

house as a conservatory, that heat is stored in the house wall. The arrangement helps to keep both house and greenhouse warmer than they would be if they were separate.

Both Original and Design Permaculture can reduce the need for work and other inputs in the garden, make a positive ecological impact, and increase yields. They're not mutually exclusive – both can be combined in the same garden but equally you can have one without the other.

How to Apply Original Permaculture to the Garden

No-Dig Gardening

In a natural ecosystem, disturbed or bare soil is very rare. An undisturbed soil, covered with plant material, either living or dead, is protected from erosion and free to develop its natural fertility. Moving and exposing the soil disrupts the biological processes of fertility and leads to the loss of precious organic matter.

So why do we dig our gardens? The main reason is to relieve compaction, and the main cause of compaction is treading on the soil. If a garden is laid out on a bed system, gardening without digging becomes a possibility. A bed system consists of

Maddy and Tim Harland's no dig, permaculture food forest.

beds alternating with paths, with the beds sufficiently narrow that every part of them can be reached from a path. The gardener never needs to tread on the growing area, so there is no compaction.

Doing away with digging saves a lot of work. What's more, although quite a large proportion of the garden is composed of paths, the overall yield is usually higher than in a traditional vegetable plot. In part this is because the vegetables can be placed equidistant at their ideal spacing in both dimensions. Without a bed system they must be planted in rows, to allow space for the gardener to walk between them, so they're too close to each other in one dimension and too far apart in the other.

No-dig is not a dogma. Sometimes it may be worthwhile to dig, perhaps to remove perennial weeds or to mix in compost in a raw soil. But these occasions should be rare in most gardens.

Perennials

In nature, mature ecosystems are composed almost entirely of perennial plants, that is plants which live for many years, in contrast to most of our vegetables which are annuals and only live for one year. There are advantages for us in imitating this aspect of natural ecosystems.

Anyone who has grown both fruit and vegetables will know how much less work it takes to grow the fruit, which is perennial, compared to the vegetables, which need to be raised from seed each year. But there are a number of perennial vegetables, and other vegetables, that can maintain themselves in the garden by self-seeding.

Most perennials are more resistant to pests and diseases than annuals, and once they're established they're too big to be troubled by slugs. Since they keep the ground covered for all the growing season, weeds hardly get a look-in.

One of the most useful perennial vegetables is Daubenton's perennial kale. Easily grown from cuttings, it can give you abundant greens all year round with hardly any attention. Sea beet, the perennial form of leaf beet, gives its yield of spinach leaves mainly in the spring, when there are few annuals available for picking. Leaf beet and its sister Swiss chard are among the most successful self-seeders, while rocket, land cress and lamb's lettuce will self-seed readily to give salad greens. There's a wide range of perennial onions, including Welsh and tree onions and wild garlic. (See page 89 for more information on perennials.)

Polycultures

Diversity is one of the most familiar characteristics of natural ecosystems. Organic gardeners know the value of it, both as the key to reducing pest and disease problems, and in making more complete use of the soil nutrients, as each crop has slightly different needs. They achieve diversity mainly by means of crop rotation, which gives diversity through time. In permaculture we go a step further by working with simultaneous diversity too.

Growing a mix of vegetables in one bed usually takes more care and attention than growing a single crop, but the rewards can be great. Not only do the different plants use different parts of the nutrient resource, but the fact that they have different shapes, grow at different speeds and at different times of the year means that they can share the resources of space and time as well. So the overall yield is higher for the same resource base.

For example, if short, bushy lettuce is planted between tall, thin garlic neither significantly shades the other, and if the timing's right the garlic will be harvested before the lettuce has taken up all the space. Squashes and sweet corn have the same relationship in terms of space, though not in time. Cabbage and lettuce are more similar in structure but lettuce is faster growing. If the two are planted alternately, the lettuce can be removed when the cabbage is only half grown, thus making use of the empty ground between the young cabbage plants. In summertime, low-growing salad plants, such as lamb's lettuce and purslane, can actually benefit from a little shade from taller plants in a mixed bed.

The more complex the mixture the more skill and attention it takes to grow it. If there are many different crops in the bed rather than just two, you need to watch it constantly and keep selectively harvesting and thinning as the plants mature at different rates. But the rewards can be correspondingly greater. Whether to grow

Michael Guerra's garden, showing productive use of small space.

garden polycultures or not depends on your priorities. They're most worthwhile if you have a small garden and want to get the maximum yield out of it. If your priority is simplicity and ease of management, single crops are probably best.

Stacking

In almost every part of the Earth where growing conditions are good enough, the natural vegetation is a multi-layered forest of trees, shrubs and herbaceous plants. Natural grassland is only found where rainfall is lacking, and it generally produces much less biomass per year than forest.

Yet most of our food-producing systems, whether on farms or in gardens, resemble grassland, inasmuch as they are a single layer of herbaceous plants. Multi-layer systems, such as the forest garden mentioned above, invariably yield more food. Although each layer may yield less than it would if grown alone, the overall yield is higher.

In permaculture we call multi-layer growing 'stacking'. Growing vegetables of different heights, as in some of the examples of polyculture given above, is stacking on a small-scale. In general stacking is a matter of thinking in three dimensions, of seeing a garden as a volume of space rather than just a surface area. So using any vertical

Stacking.
Above: peas and spinach below wineberries.
Below: sweet peas, beans and lettuce.

space – such as walls, fences, window boxes and balconies – for growing can be seen as a form of stacking.

The availability of light is the main limitation on stacking. Open-grown trees in the middle of a small garden, especially one surrounded by buildings or other trees, will leave little light for the lower layers. So in most small gardens the walls and fences around the edges offer the main opportunity for stacking. Fruit trees, most soft fruits and a few vegetables can be trained up walls and fences, hardly impeding the light that reaches the main body of the garden and taking up very little horizontal space.

Fruit trees can be trained as espaliers, fans or cordons. The yield per square metre of horizontal space is higher than for any other method of fruit tree culture. All the cane fruits, plus red currants and gooseberries, can be wall-trained. The hybrid berries are particularly useful; one of my favourites is the veitchberry (loganberry), which gives its yield in the gap between summer raspberries and blackberries.

The choice of climbing vegetables is rather limited. It includes some varieties of squashes and cucumbers, climbing beans and tall varieties of pea. The fact that these all come from two families makes a climbing rotation hard to design. But other tall plants, such as sweet corn, tomatoes and sunflowers, can be included.

Succession

The down side of wall-trained fruit trees is that they need more intensive care than open-grown fruit trees. Where very low maintenance is a priority, open-grown trees may be a better choice. Of course these will eventually cast quite a bit of shade, but in the early years a series of edible crops can be grown beneath them. This mimics the natural succession which takes place as a natural ecosystem regenerates on bare ground: the first colonists are annual plants, followed by herbaceous perennials, followed by shrubs and trees.

At first annual vegetables can be grown between the young trees which will also benefit from the manuring, watering and attention given to the vegetables, without significantly reducing their yield. As the trees grow, the annuals can be replaced with perennial vegetables. Most of these are more tolerant of shade and root competition than are annuals. Also, since they take less effort to grow, any reduction in yield as the trees get bigger may be more acceptable. When the trees are mature they can be under planted with shade-tolerant perennials such as wild garlic.

Alternatively, in a large garden where full-sized standard fruit trees have been planted, soft fruit can be grown between them in the early years. The soft fruit will come to the end of its productive life at about the time when the trees start to bear a reasonable crop.

Mimicking natural succession in this way makes for a garden that is constantly abundant through the years, as the focus of production moves from the lower layers to the upper ones.

How to Apply Design Permaculture to the Garden

Design Permaculture doesn't necessarily imitate natural ecosystems in such a literal way. It uses an understanding of how natural ecosystems work to guide how we grow food, or meet any of our other needs.

The key to what makes ecosystems work is the fact that all its components self-select to work in harmony with each other. The plants and animals are perfectly suited to the environments where they are found within the ecosystem, and they help each other thrive by a network of mutually beneficial relationships.

For example, different plants specialise in extracting different minerals from the soil. These minerals become available to other plants through leaf fall or the death of the plant, by the action of the micro-organisms which decompose them. Trees give shelter and humidity to plants that need these conditions, while many animals disperse the seeds of plants, often in return for a meal of fruit.

In the Garden

Translated to a garden, this principle of beneficial relationships means carefully placing things in the situation where they will function best. The different components of the garden – vegetables, fruit trees, compost heap, greenhouse and so on – may look just the same as those in any other garden. What makes it a permaculture garden is the fact that they have been thoughtfully arranged so there is a maximum of beneficial relationships.

For a start this means placing things in relation to the physical environment. Thus sun-loving plants and the greenhouse are best placed in the sunniest part of the garden, while shade-tolerant plants and other things which don't need sun, such as the compost heap, can go in shady places. It also means placing things in relation to each other, for example, planting tall, wind-hardy plants where they can give shelter to more wind-sensitive ones.

Just as important is placing things in relation to the needs and energies of the people who use the garden. The clearest example of this is in a long narrow garden, where traditionally the vegetables are put at the far end, well away from the house. But it's much easier to give the vegetables the attention they need if they are close at hand where you see them as part of your daily round.

Vegetables placed within sight of the kitchen window are both easier to grow and yield more than those that are out of sight. This has been the experience of many gardeners who have had their vegetable patch both close by and further away at different times.

All of this may seem like common sense, and it is. Any wise and experienced gardener will consider these factors when laying out their garden. What permaculture design offers is a simple framework in which any gardener, including beginners, can work out the best possible arrangement for their garden right from the start.

This will not only make the garden more productive in the long run, but save a great deal of unnecessary labour. Once we have set up our garden most of us can't face the task of rearranging it. If the original design was less than optimum, we then spend years accepting lower productivity and extra work. A job that takes an extra couple of minutes each time you do it means many hours wasted over the years.

The pleasure we get from the garden in terms of beauty and recreation is just as important a 'yield' from the garden as food production. The relative importance of each will depend on the wishes of the individual family. Ecological impact must also be considered.

This includes both providing wildlife habitat and considering the wider impact of the garden. For example, collecting rainwater and composting waste paper and card will reduce both the resources used and the output of pollution.

Knowing Your Garden

The most important thing is not to rush straight into making decisions about the garden. Our first impulse is usually to say, "let's turn the whole thing into a forest garden!" or "Let's have a pond over there". But this is putting the cart before the horse. A really effective design can only come after careful observation and listening.

The best way to observe and record the physical aspects of the garden is to make a map of what is there already, a 'base map'. You may not feel this is necessary. But design is all to do with the use of space, and it's impossible to design anything more than a haphazard way without a reasonably accurate scale map. Equally important, you really get to know the garden by mapping it. The act of mapping makes us much more observant than we normally are. I often find that ideas start to flow during the rather mechanical but concentrated work of drawing a map.

It's a good idea to photocopy this map and use it as a template for future maps. One other map which is usually well worthwhile is a version showing where the wind comes from, where the sunny and shady places are and so on, in other words, the microclimates of the garden. This is vital information, and ideally it should be collected over a whole year so you get to note all the changes with the seasons.

This may seem a long time to wait before really getting started, but it's well worth it. In the meantime you can still use the garden as it has been up to now and grow any annual plants you choose, but without doing anything that commits you to permanent change, like planting trees or building structures. The more time you have to consider it, the better your design will be in the long run.

Knowing What You Want

You may think you already know what you want from your garden. But, just like making a map, making a list of your wants over a period of time helps to make sure that nothing is missed. Every member of the family must be asked.

It's important at this stage to keep basic wants. For example, you may initially say, "I want a forest garden". Well, why do you want a forest garden? Are you particularly fond of fruit, or is it the low maintenance requirement of a forest garden that appeals to you? Perhaps you just like the idea of a complex ecosystem developing in your back garden. Any one of these needs can be met in a number of ways, of which a forest garden is only one.

As well as listing the outputs you want, you need to put down what inputs you can give the garden. These include: how much time you're realistically prepared to spend gardening over the years, how much work you're prepared to do putting your design into action in the first place, how much money you have to spend, and what skills you have or can acquire.

Decisions

Before coming to any firm decisions, it is necessary to evaluate what you have, both in the garden itself and on your wish list.

Which of the plants and structures already in the garden do you most want to keep, and which do you most want to get rid of? Where are the best growing areas, both in terms of microclimate and soil, and in terms of being close to your centre of attention?

As for your wish list, you may have too much on it for the space available, or for the amount of work you and your family are able to do. If so, you need to rank the things you want in order of priority.

At this stage you only have raw data. Turning it into a coherent design can seem a bit daunting, but you don't have to come up with the final design in one day. The best approach is to make several photocopies of your base map and sketch a few alternative concepts for the garden on this.

Which of these makes the best use of the space, microclimates and soils of the garden? How well does each of them meet your needs? Bit by bit the ideal layout will emerge.

Remember that you don't need to implement your design all at once. An important part of the design process is to come up with a staged implementation plan, perhaps spread over several years. Match it to the rate of work you find easy and pleasurable.

You may change your mind about some aspects of your design as you implement it, or after you've finished. This is fine. It's all part of the evolution of a good garden. The important thing is to get the main framework of the garden right before you start, so any changes will be minor and easy to make. The big decisions are almost always the most important ones.

An Example

I take my own garden as an example of the design process, but not as an ideal permaculture garden. There is no such thing. The whole point of permaculture design is that each garden will be unique, tailored to the specific place and people. This is a brief summary of the design, but I trust it's enough to illustrate how the process I've outlined above can work in practice.

An example of design. Here Tim Harland shows their forest garden design, 25 years ago (top). Below is is how it looks now.

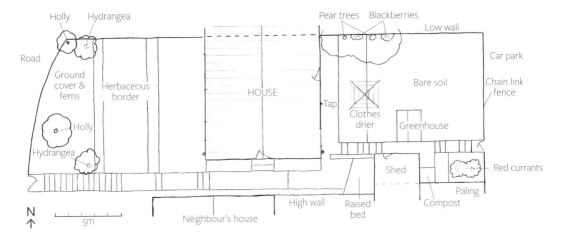

Base map.

The Garden

The base map (above) shows the garden as it was when we arrived here, and the design map (facing page) shows the proposed changes. Being a sloping site (back garden to front), a profiled drawing was also prepared but is not shown here for simplicity.

The garden is on a west-facing hill top, and the front garden, to the west of the house, was very exposed to wind. Late frosts are not a problem. The only seriously shady parts of the garden are along the southern edge. The soil is uniform throughout the garden and reasonably fertile. Sources of water are as shown on the base map. There's an excellent view of the countryside from the western windows. The back garden was overlooked from the north, east and south-west. In addition to the garden we have a field some distance away, where we have since planted a little orchard.

Our Wants

There are two of us, my wife Cathy and I. Her overall vision for the garden was of a combination of beauty and food production; mine was of food production combined with low maintenance. Specific things we wanted included: to grow greens, salads and soft fruit; to have enough lawn to sit out on with a group of up to eight people; to have an attractive view of the garden from all four windows, and to the south of the lawn (since you tend to sit facing the sun); and privacy. Also, I was particularly interested in growing perennial vegetables.

Our work took us away from home for long periods, including a regular fortnight in May, which put a limit on the amount of annual vegetables we could grow. When at home I would usually spend a couple of hours a week in the garden, and sometimes a whole day. I'm a reasonably competent gardener.

What We Decided

In evaluating the garden, we decided: to keep all the existing plants; the existing feature we most valued was the long view to the west; the thing we most wanted to change was the excessively rectangular appearance of the garden; and we needed a

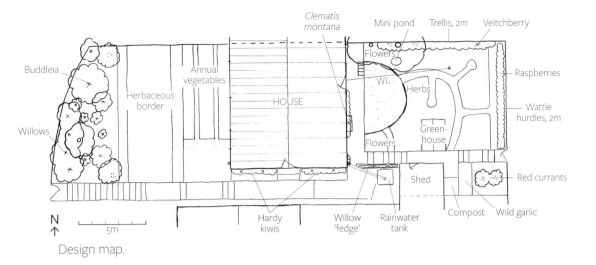

Design map.

Buddleia

Herbaceous
border

Annual
vegetables

Willows

Clematis
montana

Mini pond   Trellis, 2m   Veitchberry

Flowers

HOUSE

WL

Herbs

Raspberries

Green-
house

Wattle
hurdles, 2m

Flowers

Shed

Red currants

Compost   Wild garlic

N

5m

Hardy
kiwis

Willow
'fedge'

Rainwater
tank

direct route from the back door to the back garden. We felt that all the items on our wish list were realistic in the circumstances.

We decided against any structural changes to the front garden, but considered three possible concepts for the back. I made enlarged photocopies of the back garden from the base map and sketched on them in pencil. One concept had the lawn where it was but changed to a semi-circular shape, one had a circular lawn in the middle, and the other had the lawn at the far end. As you can see from the design map, we chose the first of these. Not only did we like it best, but it required the least work to implement.

The design map shows how we designed for privacy and beauty while leaving plenty of space for food crops. The extreme western section of the garden became a combined wildlife area and windbreak. This included the trees and shrubs which were there plus self-seeded ash trees and planted willows and buddleia. Annual pollarding and coppicing kept it at the right height to provide shelter for the front garden vegetables without blocking the view. We have made a few minor changes since then, notably moving the greenhouse further to the east. But overall the design has worked really well.

Service to the Planet

You may well ask how this kind of permaculture design contributes to sustainability. It does enable you to plan ecological features into your garden right from the start, but that is not its main contribution.

The biggest single component of our ecological footprint is the ecological cost of our food. Most of this cost is not in the growing of it but in its transport, distribution and processing. Growing our own fresh food at home eliminates most of the costs. Permaculture design can make home gardening easier, more pleasant and more productive. If this leads to us growing some of our food at home, or growing more of it than we would in a poorly designed garden, it's of great service to the planet.

Personal transport makes up another big chunk of our ecological footprint. If good design makes our gardens sufficiently pleasant places to spend time in so we make fewer car trips, so much the better for the Earth.

A sunny orchard for apples and pears that creates part shade for understorey plants like comfrey.

2

How to Garden Successfully in the Sun or Shade

There are many different things that affect plant growth, including soil conditions, climatic conditions such as temperature and moisture, pests and diseases, competition from weeds and so on. We do our best to provide ideal conditions, but the one that is usually most difficult to change is the amount of light the plants get. Most domestic gardens are relatively shady, or at least parts of them are. The key to success is to observe which are the sunniest and shadiest parts of the garden and place different plants according to the amount of light they need.

Plants need light in order to grow, and most food plants do best in full sun. In fact the miracle of photosynthesis, in which plants turn sunlight into food, is the absolute basis of all life on Earth. Sunlight also brings warmth and dries out both soil and plants. So there's a complexity of factors to consider, and not every plant necessarily does best in the sunniest position. Having said that, nothing does well in really deep shade. This is the place to put the non-living components of the garden, like the compost heap, a movable shed or water storage.

But leafy greens and salad plants can actually do better in a shady part of the garden than in a sunnier part. The heat and dryness of a sunny spot encourage flowering rather than leaf production. Also, since leaves are solar collectors they respond to low light levels by growing bigger, and a moderate level of shade can actually be beneficial.

Vegetables with smaller leaves, like carrots, prefer as much sunshine as they can get. Those that only produce their crop after flowering, such as squashes and beans, also need a sunny environment to encourage insects for pollination. The problem with these annual vegetables is that if you're growing them on rotation they will all be in the sunny and shady part of the garden in one year or another. To my mind this is just one of the benefits of growing perennial vegetables. In fact some authorities on organic gardening say that rotation is not really worthwhile in a small domestic garden. In that case placing different crops where they will do best may be a better option.

Herbs growing in the greenhouse.   Alpine strawberries in a sunny spot.

As for fruits, as a rule of thumb dessert varieties of top (tree) fruits need full sun, while most cooking varieties and most soft (bush and cane) fruits can do well in a position where they get half a day's sunlight. This is because dessert fruits need to ripen more fully, and the shrubby fruits are descended from woodland shrubs which have always had to cope with the shade cast by the trees above. An exception is autumn fruiting raspberry, which ripens later in the year when there is less light overall, and needs full sun.

The table lists most of the common edible plants that can cope with partial shade.

Another option for shady places is ornamentals. The ambition of every plant is simply to grow big enough to have the strength to flower and set seed. But we're asking our food plants to produce unnaturally large yields of leaves, roots or fruits – more than they need simply to reproduce. Thus they need the best conditions we can give them, in terms of soil and water as well as light and warmth. This is not so with ornamentals, though of course some of them come from sunny climates and do need full sun.

The sunniest parts of the garden are likely to be the warmest too, especially where the sunlight is reflected back onto the soil by a south-facing wall. This is especially important for winter and spring crops, as the pictures of autumn-sown broad beans show.

A disadvantage of sunny walls is that the soil at the base is always drier than elsewhere in the garden. This can be an advantage for the aromatic herbs, most of which come from the Mediterranean, where a summer drought is the norm. They not only grow well in such a situation but produce more of their essential oils, which is what we grow them for.

Fruits, on the other hand, really need water in the summer. So fruit that is grown up a wall, even a relatively shady one, needs to be planted 30-40cm (12-16in) away and trained back onto the wall.

It pays to take some time getting to know your garden, really knowing where the sunny and shady places are. It can be worth making a map at different times of the year, hatching in the areas that are in shade in the morning, noon and afternoon. Thus the really shady places get double- or treble-hatched. One in spring and one in summer should be enough. These can be superimposed on each other and then you'll really see which are the shady parts and which the sunny.

Indirect light is important. A north-facing wall may be a good place for morello cherries or soft fruit if there are no obstructions nearby. But if there are shrubs or structures that stop it getting much indirect light it may not. For winter and spring crops there's a big difference between the seasonal shade of deciduous trees and the constant shade of buildings and evergreens. In fact deciduous trees can be a help, as their twigs help to conserve heat at ground level and frost can be less frequent and less severe beneath them. But a disadvantage of all trees is that they compete for water and nutrients with anything growing near them, and the soil beneath a big tree or vigorous hedge is always drier than out in the open, especially in summer.

Some Shade Tolerant Edibles					
6-8 Hours, Sun in Summer			4-6 Hours, Sun in Summer		
Herbs	Vegetables	Fruit	Herbs	Vegetables	Fruit
Fennel	Autumn and winter cabbage	Alpine strawberries	Bay	Calabrese	Cooking gooseberries
Rosemary		Blackcurrants	Chives	Chard	Loganberries
Sage	Beetroot	Cooking apples	Horseradish	Cress	Morello cherries
Thyme	Brussels sprouts	Desert gooseberries	Mint	Kale	Red currants
	Cauliflower		Parsley	Kohl rabi	Rhubarb
	Early carrots	Kiwi fruit		Lettuce	
	Leeks	Raspberries		Most leafy perennials	
	Onion sets	White currants		Radish	
	Parsnips			Spinach	
	Peas			Spring cabbage	
	Potatoes			Welsh and tree onions	
	Runner beans				
	Small tomatoes				
	Sprouting broccoli				
	Turnips				

A vegetable polyculture of red cabbage, beans and sweet corn.

3

The Minimalist Garden

O ver the past few years I have developed a style of gardening that suits me well, though it looks a little unconventional. A friend who visited for lunch one day was a bit mystified when, colander in hand, we approached what looked like a jumble of wild plants to pick a salad. In a few moments we had filled the colander with a mix of tasty leaves. He looked quite surprised and said, "I see you have a minimalist garden."

The name has stuck. Based on perennial and self-seeding vegetables, including some wild ones, it is a garden that requires very little input, yet it can put a salad or a pot of greens on the table any day of the year. It is the kind of garden that has often been associated with the name permaculture in the past. Of course permaculture is not synonymous with any one style of gardening. In a good permaculture design, the gardening methods are chosen to fit the individual gardener and the individual site: and that is just how my style of gardening arose.

My work takes me away from home, often for a couple of weeks at a time, and often at important times in the gardening calendar. Perennials and self-seeders fit this pattern well, because once the garden is established there is very little work to do, and a fortnight's absence in, say, the middle of May is not the disaster it would be in an annual vegetable garden. In addition, after some years of chronic illness, my physical strength is not that great, so anything that reduces the amount of work is welcome.

The main influence on the site was slugs. I was gardening in a place so sluggy that it was impossible to grow most kinds of annual vegetables without massive and constant use of slug pellets – which I will not do. On the whole the perennial and self-seeding vegetables are less highly bred than the annuals, and have not had all of their natural resistance bred out of them. Also, perennials do not have to pass through the vulnerable seedling stage every year, as annuals do. A minimalist garden is not immune to slugs and snails, but it is highly resistant.

Site Layout

All vegetables need a fertile soil in order to yield well, but if you plan to have both a conventional annual garden and a minimalist garden, the annuals should get first priority on the most fertile soil. They are high input/high output plants compared to

Patrick's minimalist garden.

the perennials and self-seeders, and you want to be sure of a return on all the work you put into them. Heavy clays are only really suitable for a minimalist garden if they are well structured and well drained, because of course there will be no digging.

As for light, perennials and self-seeders need as much as annuals, but not necessarily at the same time of year. Many self-seeders do most of their growing in autumn and spring. Perennials, which spend the winter as a mature rootstock or complete plant, can put on a lot of growth early in the spring, when annuals are still seeds in the seed packet or at most seedlings in a seed tray. This means the plants in a minimalist garden are doing much of their growing before trees come into leaf. Most of them can be grown successfully in the shade of deciduous fruit trees, as long as they get some indirect light from the side. In fact a minimalist vegetable garden is very much the same thing as the ground layer of an edible woodland garden.

Many self-seeding vegetables, including some perennial ones, can be invasive if given the opportunity. They do not get this in a minimalist garden, where most of the space is occupied by vigorous perennial plants. But in an annual vegetable garden there is plenty of bare soil for much of the year, and they can spread into it like weeds. So minimalist and annual gardens should not ideally be sited side by side.

A minimalist garden needs regular attention, if only to note which of the wide variety of plants is ready to eat, so it should not be sited in some out-of-the-way corner.

Clockwise from top: Young leeks, purple climbing beans, squash, broad beans and garlic.

It can be designed to look attractive, by careful arrangement of vegetables with contrasting leaf texture and shape, and by the inclusion of a few flowers, many of which are edible.

Since this is a no-dig garden it needs to be laid out on a bed system, i.e. with a network of paths so that it is never necessary to walk on the growing area. I have used both keyhole beds and the conventional straight beds. The shape of the site and existing paths may suggest one or the other.

A scattering of perennial flowers, such as sweet Williams, wild foxgloves (though they are poisonous) and Michaelmas daisies brighten up the garden. As for fruit, both soft fruit and young trees can be included. One of the best choices is hybrid berries – loganberries, tayberries and so on – trained up the fences around the garden.

I always grow a few easy annuals on the side. My favourites are broad beans and garlic, both autumn sown, both pretty impervious to slugs and other pests. Where slugs are not too much of a problem, runner beans and squashes give an excellent return on the work invested in them, though you do need plenty of space for squash. The perennials and self-seeders are mainly leaf vegetables, so beans and squash add variety to the home-grown produce. They can be rotated with self-seeders, or grown in a separate part of the garden, but then other kinds must be included to give a good rotation.

Perennials and Self-Seeders

If you already grow a garden of annual vegetables you will find a minimalist garden complements it very well. Perennials put on plenty of leaf early in spring – since they start the year as a mature plant rather than a seed – and they are in full production during the 'hungry gap' from March to May, when even the best growers of annual vegetables have little to eat in their gardens. Later in the season, when the annuals are in full production, many of the perennials go to seed and their leaves become smaller and in some cases less tasty. The self-seeders are mostly hardy salad plants, giving green leaves in winter and spring when conventional salads are scarce.

Perennials form the backbone of a minimalist garden. They can be very productive, and once established they need very little maintenance. Big leafy ones like Good King Henry, perennial kale and sea beet hardly even need weeding, as they shade out many of the weeds. Self-seeders require a bit more work. They need open ground to seed into, and where they can seed, so can unwanted plants. As well as weeding they sometimes need thinning to get the best from them. But they add greatly to the variety of plants that can be grown, especially for salad.

Vegetables and Herbs

The distinction between vegetables and herbs is a fairly artificial one. A herb is really just a vegetable with a particularly strong taste or medicinal property which we take in relatively small quantities. In practice there is a continuum from the very strong tasting to the very bland, and there are many plants towards the middle of the range that we often call herbs but which can be included in salads or cooked dishes in fairly large quantities. In fact it is possible to make a delicious salad entirely of 'herbs'. The secret is to include as many different kinds as possible: the greater the variety the better the taste.

Since a minimalist garden is mainly composed of perennial and self-seeding vegetables, there is little chance to get rid of perennial weeds once the garden is established, so it's a good idea to start with as clean a sheet as possible.

The best way to sort out a serious perennial weed problem is to put down a light-excluding mulch, such as recycled black plastic, for a time before planting. Ideally it should be down for a whole spring and summer, as it only kills plants when they try to grow. But it can be moderately effective over winter, especially if the winter is a mild one, killing all the annual weeds and less persistent perennials, but leaving patches of tougher perennials such as couch to be dug in spring.

Where the weeds are annuals, or young perennials, a grow-through mulch can be used. Here a biodegradable light-excluding layer, such as cardboard or newspaper, is weighed down with a layer of manure and, in dry weather, topped off with a layer of straw. Holes are made in the mulch, and young vegetable plants are planted in pockets of soil placed over the holes. The effectiveness of the mulch depends on the vegetables growing well and out-competing the weeds that start to grow as the mulch decomposes.

If there is any compaction in the upper layers of the soil it can be broken up before planting by pushing a garden fork into the soil to its full depth and heaving on it to open

These squash and potato plants have been grown on top of a mulch of cardboard and manure to get rid of the mass of nettles beneath.

up the soil. Compaction in the subsoil can be relieved by double digging – a big job, not to be undertaken unless absolutely necessary. A slower-acting alternative is to build a deep bed on top and allow the perennial plants to drill through the compacted soil with their tap roots, along with the fat earthworms you will grow in the deep mulch layer.

Many perennials can be bought as plants, which saves time but is much more expensive. Whether you raise the plants yourself or buy them in, planting out has one great advantage over direct seeding: transplants are less vulnerable to slugs than tiny seedlings are. It is much easier to keep a little cold frame free of slugs than to protect seedlings as they come up in the open garden. Most perennial vegetables can be sown in the spring and planted out a couple of months later, but the individual requirements of different kinds should be given on the seed packet.

Self-seeders can usually be sown direct, but where slugs are severe, self-sown plants often escape when hand-sown ones get eaten. So it can be worth establishing the self-seeders from transplants too.

On the whole a polyculture works best planted in drifts: small groups of each kind of plant, rather than individual plants mixed together. This means each plant can be given its preferred spacing, which is not possible when big plants are mixed up with little ones. It also makes it easier to put each kind in its ideal environment relative to the garden environment and the other plants.

Enjoying Your Garden

Once established, a minimalist garden takes very little work: it's more like steering a boat than rowing one.

Little weeding is needed between vigorous perennials, especially if mulch is used. When plants die down in winter, extra mulch can be spread to protect the bare soil. It is not really necessary to make compost: kitchen scraps can be spread thinly on the soil and covered with a little mulch. Other plant foods, such as comfrey, can also be applied on the surface. I find my main pest and disease control activity is watching the ladybirds and their larvae eat the aphids.

Self-seeders take a little more work than perennials. Ground needs to be cleared for them to seed into, and some weeding and thinning may be needed when they come up. Alternatively, if they come up thick they can be harvested as a cut-and-come-again or seedling crop, or even treated as a green manure. Each year one or two healthy plants should be left with plenty of space to grow and not picked, so they can put all their energy into seed production.

Apart from that, all is harvesting! Some of the plants have unfamiliar tastes, and a bit of experimentation can be well worthwhile. For example, Good King Henry (*Chenopodiaceae bonus-henricus*) has a slightly bitter overtone when boiled or steamed on its own. But when blended with carrots in a stir-fry, it gives a rich, savoury taste that is absolutely delicious.

Raised beds planted in drifts of carrots, spinach and perennial kale.

Raised beds built with coppiced chestnut to bring the beds within comfortable reach for someone with arthritis.

4

Raised Bed Gardening

The soil is not an inert mineral medium; it's a vibrant ecosystem, full of billions of creatures ranging from microscopic bacteria to the mighty earthworm. If we come along with a spade and turn it upside down we do as much damage to that ecosystem as an earthquake does to a human city. Many of the little creatures that work so hard to make the soil fertile die in the cataclysm. Earthworms are exposed to birds and are picked off one by one. Far too much air enters the soil and the excess of oxygen which it brings burns up the humus, which is so vital to soil fertility. In short, digging wrecks natural soil fertility and leaves us with the task of rebuilding it by our own efforts.

Why would anyone do such a thing? Well, there are a number of reasons why people do it, but the most important one is usually to relieve soil compaction. The most common cause of soil compaction is treading on the soil, especially when it's moist or wet. So the essential prerequisite for no-dig gardening is a system that enables you to tend your plants without ever treading on the soil where they're growing. This is exactly what the bed system does for you.

Flat Beds

The simplest kind of bed is a flat, straight bed. All you do is lay out your garden in alternating strips of bed and path. All the growing takes place on the beds, all the treading on the paths, and never the twain shall meet. The width of the bed can be tailored to the individual gardener. The idea is that you should be able to easily reach the middle of each bed from the path on either side. The paths should be just wide enough so you can comfortably stand or squat facing the beds to tend the plants. Typically beds are 1.2m (4ft) wide and paths 30-45cm (12-18in). The narrower the paths, the less area of unproductive land you have in the garden. Unless the beds are very long you won't need to get a wheelbarrow along the paths, and a wheelbarrow path across the end of the beds should be enough.

Raised Beds

Raised beds have a number of advantages over flat beds. The basic raised bed is made by removing the topsoil from the paths and putting it on the beds. You don't need

One example of raised beds.

Another example using log rolls as the main structure.

topsoil on the paths because you're not going to grow anything there, so you might as well give your growing area the extra fertility that comes with deeper topsoil. In fact on many soils, flat beds turn into raised beds of their own accord, as the paths get compacted by the gardener's feet while the beds get ever softer and more fluffy as compost is added and the growing earthworm population improves the structure. The increased depth of topsoil is the main advantage of raised beds over flat ones. Another is that drainage is improved and the soil dries out more quickly after rain. This is a great help in the wet climate of Britain.

In drier climates, where extra drying is the last thing you want, flat beds are better, and even sunken ones may be worthwhile. Another advantage of raised beds is that they can be that bit warmer on a frosty night. Cold air sinks, and it will drain off into the paths leaving the tops of the beds distinctly warmer. Raised beds are also a bit more permanent than flat ones. With beds and paths on the same level the exact position of the paths can get lost, and then you can find yourself trying to grow vegetables in the compacted soil of a path. A sunken path is much more of a fixture.

Layout

An advantage shared by all kinds of beds is that they can make rotation planning easier. For example, if you use a four year rotation and have eight beds, it's very easy to see what goes where each year. Obviously this works best in a regular-shaped garden where it's easy to lay out beds that are all the same size. The simplest layout is one with straight beds, but all sorts of curves are possible as long as you keep to the golden rule that every part of every bed must be reachable from a path.

Curves are great in a domestic garden, where a pleasing appearance can be as important as the yield of food and ease of working. But on larger areas, especially in a market garden, straight lines make life much easier. Straight beds can also be useful where you want to make maximum use of a small rectangular space. If the beds are long it can be useful to have a cross path halfway down the block of beds so you can get to both sides of a bed without having to go right round the end. This isn't a problem throughout the year because you can step on the soil as long as it's reasonably dry. It's treading on wet soil that causes compaction. If you don't want to have a cross path you can put in stepping stones to allow you to cross over the bed. When you place a stepping stone, make sure it's well proud of the soil surface. Your weight will press it down in time and if it starts out flush with the soil it can disappear beneath the surface in a year or two. Stepping stones really come into their own in an irregular curvy layout. This kind of design often results in beds of varying width that can't all be reached from a path. A combination of paths and stepping stones can give you more design freedom than paths alone.

Edging and Paths

A little retaining wall of bricks or planks along the edges will help to keep the beds neat and stop soil from falling down into the paths, but it's not necessary. In fact I wouldn't recommend it because these are just the places that slugs and snails love to hide. Giving the bed a gently rounded profile with sloping edges does away with the need for edging. Some thought needs to be given to how to manage the paths. Any plant life that grows in them can spread into the beds and thus become a weed. The best solution is mulching. Woodchip can be effective, especially with a layer of cardboard underneath it. This will need replacing from time to time and a more long-term solution is strips of carpet, placed upside down. Carpets made entirely out of artificial fibres are the most durable, but avoid ones with foam rubber backing, which soon disintegrate due to sunlight and makes a mess. (Editor's note: Pure wool carpets are best for mulching as a lot of non-wool carpets contain chemicals that are best avoided.)

Yields

Some people might be put off the bed system because of the high proportion of the garden used up by paths. Surely this means the overall yield must be lower? It could do if it weren't for a number of factors that work in favour of the bed system. The lack of soil compaction and the lack of any need for destructive digging both make for a more fertile soil. So does the fact that all compost and manure can be concentrated on the soil where the plants are actually growing. We've already seen the drainage and microclimate advantages of raised beds, and an added advantage is that it's very easy to fit mini-polytunnels over individual beds. Without the bed system you have to leave space between the plants to walk along when you're tending them. This means the plants must be grown in rows. When they're in rows, plants are too close together in one dimension and too far apart in the other. That means that, firstly, they start competing with each other earlier in the season than they otherwise would, and, secondly, space remains unused between them till later in the season. Equidistant spacing avoids both of these problems and gives maximum yields, and on beds there's nothing to stop you planting at equidistant spacing. It also means that the soil gets covered earlier in the season and weeds are suppressed more effectively. The net result of this is that the overall yield of a garden laid out on the bed system is usually higher rather than lower than a similar garden without beds.

The beds can be straight, for ease of working, or curved, for a more attractive design. But there are many variations on this theme.

These include: high beds for ease of working, terraced beds for sloping ground, angled beds set to face the sun, beds for sites with no natural soil, and even beds for mechanised production.

Straight raised beds without edges.

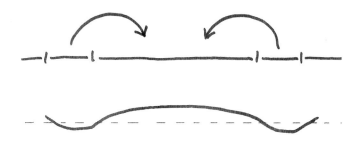

To make raised beds dig the topsoil from the paths either side
and place it in the centre.

Straight raised beds are ideally 1.2m wide with 50cm paths between.

An example of a high bed for easy access.

High Beds

The normal raised bed is only raised in as much as the topsoil is removed from the paths and placed on the beds. It may require slightly less bending on the part of the gardener than a bed that's flush with the path, but not much. People with a back problem, wheelchair users, or those who simply want their gardening to be easier, will need something much higher than that. Beds 60cm (2ft) high are usually about right, but ideally the height – and the width of the bed – should be tailor-made to the needs of the gardener.

Beds of this height must be contained in strong walls. Skimping on this is a false economy, as the walls will fail in a few years and have to be replaced. You really can't beat brick or block walls. Timber would need treating with chemicals, unless it's entirely composed of the heartwood of durable species such as chestnut or larch, which would make it expensive. Dry stone would leave too many homes for snails. Whatever the material used there must be good drainage, and if the subsoil is impermeable, drainage holes must be made in the bottom of the walls.

It would be wasteful to fill beds this deep entirely with topsoil and the lower part can even be filled with rubble to give good drainage where the local soil is heavy.

Terraced Beds

Where there's a slight slope on the garden, laying out the beds along the contour is enough to prevent soil erosion, but steeper slopes must be terraced. Proper terracing is a big job. You have to remove all the topsoil, cut the terraces, build retaining walls and return the topsoil to the flat areas. Fortunately this is only necessary on very steep slopes, and it's only worth it if you have absolutely nowhere else to garden. On moderate slopes, beds laid out on the contour can be turned into terraces at the cost of much less work, especially if there's a good depth of topsoil to work with.

When you first lay out the beds, place the topsoil from each path on the lower part of the bed immediately above it. The beds may need a little retaining wall of bricks, blocks, planks or logs to hold the soil in place. Unfortunately this can make an ideal hiding place for slugs. If you're in a very sluggy area, you may have to forgo retaining walls and accept the task of shovelling the slumped soil back up onto the bed every now and then.

Each time you cultivate the soil, rake a little downhill from the top edge of the bed towards the lower edge. Never move too much soil at a time, especially if the topsoil is thin, and always add extra compost to the upper edge to replace the lost fertility.

Sun-angled Beds

In most temperate climate areas the best alignment for beds is north to south, so that the sun shines on one side of the bed in the morning and on the other in the afternoon. If the beds were to run east to west, any tall growing crop would permanently shade the bed to the north of it. On a site that slopes to the north or south this will conflict with the need to place the beds on the contour. There's no hard-and-fast rule about which factor takes precedence. It depends on the relative importance of soil erosion and sunshine on the individual site. In northern areas, where the angle of the sun is low and the climate is cooler, it can be worth angling the beds towards the south. Obviously they have to lie east to west in order to do this, but the gain in solar energy can make it worthwhile. Every five degrees that the bed is tilted is the equivalent of being 80km (50 miles) further south. It can be worth angling just one bed, for early spring and late autumn crops, and leaving the rest on the flat.

Beds on Soil-less Sites

In urban areas there's sometimes no natural soil. The best solution here is often to make a raised bed on top of ground level rather than try to remove or improve what's already there. You can even make a raised bed on top of concrete as long as you ensure that excess water can drain away. This is rather like container growing and a growing medium high in organic matter will be needed.

Tomatoes growing in pots on a sunny patio. Good for easy access.

Beds for Tractors

People growing vegetables for a living are sometimes put off the idea of beds because they want to leave themselves the option of using a tractor now and then. But in fact this is no problem. The wheel track of the tractor can be adjusted to the width of the beds and you can use any mix of hand and mechanical work you choose. The advantage of not running the tractor wheels on the soil where you're actually growing your crops is even greater than not treading on it with your feet.

Container growing – tayberry, amelanchier cherry, peppermint and oregano.

A drystone path built by Patrick.

5

Building a Drystone Path

Building your own drystone path or wall is an excellent way to create a natural feature in the garden, whilst using local materials. Patrick shares some practical tips on building drystone paths, walls, steps and a simple bridge.

I love working with stone. There's great satisfaction to be had from making something useful, durable and beautiful from a local material with very few tools. Fitting the stones together is as much fun as any game or puzzle, and easy once you've grasped a few basic principles. It's one of those jobs where the end produce grows out of a blend of your intentions and the nature of the ground and the materials.

It's dry stonework I'm talking about, working without cement. The only extra material I ever bring in is the occasional bit of sand, and I use the stones I find lying about on the site. If you need to buy in stone it can be expensive, both in cash and in energy terms – stone is heavy stuff. If you live in a part of the country where there is no natural stone you need to question whether it's an appropriate material to be using in your area.

I've made paths, retaining walls, steps and once even a clapper bridge. I'll describe how to make each of these. I've never done a free standing wall, though I'd love to have a go some time, so I can't tell you how to do that. First let's look at some basic points which apply to all these projects.

Basics

The only tools you need are a spade and a garden trowel. You may possibly have use for a hammer and a flat piece of wood or a small axe. We'll come to those later. String can also be useful for laying out a line to work to.

Bigger stones make stronger structures. Always use the biggest stones you can find.

Each stone should be solid before you move on to the next. There are two ways to make a stone solid. One is to bed it into soil or sand, as in a path or the bottom course of a wall. The other is for it to rest firmly on other stones at three points. You can support it on four points, but this is much more difficult as the four supporting points have to match the underside of the new stone exactly. With three points, you can tilt the stone a fraction in order to bed it snugly. In a retaining wall or steps the third point, at the back, may be soil rather than a stone.

Having said that, a very slightly rocky stone can sometimes be tied in by the weight of stones above, but that's not ideal. A little hollow space under the middle of the stone is no bad thing.

Where stones are in contact with soil it must be well firmed, around, beneath, and between the stones. In narrow gaps use the blade of the trowel or spade, or your fingers. In wider gaps the end of the handle of a trowel or hammer work best.

If there are small tree roots these can be cut with an axe. Bigger ones are best left, to avoid damaging the tree. In that case it's best to build round the root, leaving some space for it to grow, otherwise it will disrupt your work as it swells over the years. Stones above the root should rest on other stones, not on the root.

Very occasionally it can be appropriate to hammer a stone into place, but only if you're pushing against soil rather than other stones, and if it only needs to move a little to be just right. To do this, place your flat piece of wood over the stone and hit that with the hammer. Otherwise you could crack the stone.

I never cut stones. It takes ages to do it accurately with handtools and you can always find something to fit.

Be kind to your back! Always lift stones with your back in as vertical a position as possible. Squat down and lift with your legs rather than bend over and lift with your shoulders and arms. Very heavy stones are best moved with levers.

Path

This is the easiest thing to make with stone. You dig out the soil to accommodate each stone, give it a soft bed to lie on and then put it in. Flagstones, that is flat, relatively thin stones, are best for a path. You can make a cobble path with thicker stones but it's much harder work and difficult to get a flat, smooth finish.

If you have a lovely friable soil with good crumb structure, it's not hard to give the stones a soft bed which they will settle into firmly and at just the level you want them. If you have a stiff, claggy clay it's impossible and you really have to get in some sand. Paths are the only thing I've ever used sand for.

You rarely get a good snug fit first time. If you don't, stand on the stone and rock it a bit until you see where the bed is too high, remove the stone, take out some soil or sand and replace the stone. You may need to do this several times until you get it just right. It should be well supported under its edges but a bit of hollow space can be left under the middle.

The surface of the path should be slightly higher than the surrounding soil to allow rainwater to drain off easily.

Retaining Wall

This is a wall supporting the vertical face of a terrace, very useful in a steep garden where you want to make some flat space.

The key to a strong wall is to lay your stones horizontally. A stone standing on its edge is weak and will soon be pushed out by the weight of the soil behind (Diagram A). This rule stands for all walls. Don't be misled by some modern stone walls which contain some vertical stones. These are just an outer skin of stone over an inner layer breeze block, laid with Portland cement, which sticks like glue.

The bottom course of stones should be dug into the soil by some 5-10cm (2-4in) for strength (Diagram B). Each course must tie in the one below. This means the vertical join between one stone and the next must not be directly above the join between two stones in the course below. Occasionally you can't avoid it, but even an overlap of 2cm (0.8in) is enough as long as the upper stone is resting on both of the stones below.

As you go up, make sure you have some long stones which go back into the soil of the bank so as to tie the wall into the soil (Diagram C). It's tempting to use these big stones longways on in order to make the stone go further. But this must be resisted. A wall with a clean vertical face between it and the soil will soon fall down. The upper surface of each stone should slope slightly towards the face of the wall, so that any

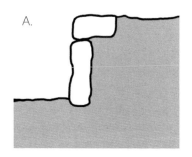

A.

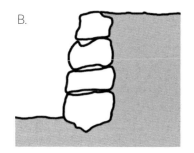

B.

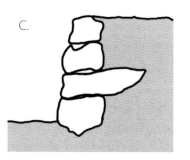

C.

A. This stone will soon be pushed out of place by the weight of soil behind it, and the wall will fall down.

B. The first stone must be partially buried.

C. A retaining wall needs to be regularly tied back into the bank.

Patrick and stonework floor and wall.

Retaining stone wall.

Stone wall used for a rockery bed.

rainwater will drain out of the wall rather than back into the soil behind. It's as well to give the wall a slight batter, that is to lean it ever so slightly back towards the bank.

Sometimes you may need to use a small stone to get a main stone to bed in properly. If there's a choice it's best to use it on the inside of the wall than on the face. At the back it can be bedded in soil and will be much stronger. Even better, if possible, is to avoid using a small stone at all by bedding the main stone directly onto soil at the back, so that the three points of support are two of stone at the front and one of soil at the back. Of course the soil must be well firmed.

Save some reasonably big stones for the top course, the coping. They need to be big because they haven't got the weight of other stones above them. Smaller, decorative stones can be laid above this, but they must be above the level of the soil or they will be pushed forward by the weight of the soil.

Detail of stones used to construct a step, showing a large stone being used to lock the smaller ones below.

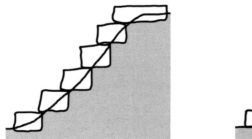

D. The length of the bottom step determines whether the steps are proud of the bank or cut into it.

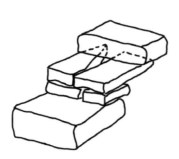

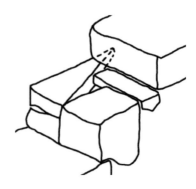

E. Making a step with smaller stones.   F. One big stone and several small ones.

Stone steps under construction. Note badly tied in upper step.

A mature flight of stone steps.

Steps

The strongest and most stable steps are made from big, rectangular stones, one for each step, long enough so that each rests on the one below. In practice that kind of stone is rarely available, but if possible stone for steps should have a roughly rectangular character. This can be reused stone which has already been shaped, or stones from a rock that naturally has bedding planes which are approximately parallel.

Steps will be stronger if they're cut into the bank rather than standing proud of it, because they will be supported by soil at the sides. This is more important if you're working with smaller stones. If you put them too far into the bank you will have to build little retaining walls either side of each step. Go just far enough in so that part of each stone is held from the side. Make the bottom step or steps longer till you find yourself cutting a bit more than filling (Diagram D).

To get a really regular flight of steps, with each one the same height and length, you need to plane it beforehand. I prefer to just start and see where the land and the materials take me. It's more fun that way and you get funkier steps.

On steep slopes, make the steps long enough from front to back. They are much more comfortable to use if they support your heel as well as your sole. It's also best if the height and length of each step is more or less the same. The surface of each step should slope slightly to the front so that they shed water.

Assuming that you haven't got the ideal massive stones, there are a number of ways of using smaller stones to make strong, stable steps.

The clapper bridge was built from two large flags with piers built into either bank and an island pier in the middle. Sadly due to deepening of the stream it has collapsed.

In general, the smaller the stones the more important it is to tie them in above, in other words to have the weight of the step above resting on them at the back (Diagram E). Note that here the shorter stones are used underneath and the longer ones, which can reach back under the step above, on top. The step is usually stronger if the upper stone is heavier than the lower.

If you have a big stone which is the right height and width for a step but not long enough you can get away without tying it in above. It should be sufficiently heavy to stay put due to its own weight. If it's the right height but not wide enough you may be able to put a long one next to it on its side, as long as this one is tied in by the step above and is firm, preferably held in by the soil at the side. But usually two stones laid flat are best (Diagram F).

Another approach is to use one big, heavy stone at the front of the step and fill in behind with smaller ones. If the big stone is really heavy the latter can be placed on their sides, well bedded into the soil and held between the big stone in front. The long axis of the smaller stones must be across the step rather than from front to back. This technique is useful where you need to put in a longer step which is above the level of the surrounding soil. It has the advantage that the stones which will be trod on are bedded into soil rather than resting on other stones.

However you arrange the stones, they need to be super-secure for a safe flight of steps. This means thinking carefully about the design. There are often several ways of using the stones you have and if you're not experienced it can be worth trying them all out until you get the best solution. It also means that wherever soil supports a stone or is used as packing between stones it needs to be rammed in very firmly.

Clapper Bridge

I've only done this once but it worked, perhaps more by luck than judgement. You need to have one very long flag, long enough to span the brook or ditch with a bit to spare at either end. You also need to support it at four points, two at either end, otherwise it will wobble. My luck was that this just happened when I built my bridge. When I placed the big stone it just sat there snugly, without a tremor when walked on. Trying to make a stone sit firmly by slipping a sliver of stone under one corner rarely works. What tends to happen is that you get that point sound and another one starts to wobble.

You also need some good heavy stones for the supporting piers, and dig them well into the soil of either bank, both downwards and back into the banks. The span of the bridge must be wide enough so the piers don't narrow the brook too much. Otherwise it can increase erosion which may undercut the piers and bring the bridge down. Sometimes a double span clapper bridge is possible, especially over a shallow brook with a bit of an island in the middle.

Cristina Crossingham's recycled urban garden.

6

Examples of Permaculture Designed Gardens

n this chapter are two examples of gardens with a permaculture influence. They have both been designed for maximum yields with a minimum input but for very different reasons.

The Recycled Urban Garden

A productive low-cost garden thriving in the shade

My sister, Cristina Crossingham,[†] lives in a terraced house in Bristol. The garden lacks space and is too shady, and when Cristina moved in it was a very soggy place. She could have bought a house with a bigger, sunnier garden but, even though she's a keen gardener, she chose this one because it's right by the Bristol to Bath cycle path. The path, on the route of an old railway, is just over the road from the house and its sides are covered in a thick growth of trees and shrubs. It doesn't only give her a verdant view; it's also part of a resource-rich landscape, which acts as an extension of her garden.

"I see my garden as part of the locality. It doesn't end at the garden gate. I can get materials for it from the neighbourhood and foraging adds to the edible produce," she says. "Wild cherries grow by the footbridge over the motorway. I can reach them with a litter picker and soon get enough for a big bowl." In its turn the garden doesn't just produce food. It's where she stores her firewood, and surplus dried rosemary that makes excellent firelighters. It's also a source of presents for friends and relations. "Cuttings are the best way of generating presents from the garden," she told me, "and chives in the spring." Her raised beds are deep, with all the topsoil from the paths and other non-growing areas of the garden added to them. The vertical sides are made

---

[†] Cristina sadly passed away in October 2016.

from concrete slabs – "people are always redoing their patios" – and slightly broken slates from a renovation project in Bristol docks. The paths are mainly made of bricks, given away at the tip, with sea pebbles on the less trodden margins as a visual contrast. The delight she takes in the creative use of found materials is evident in the appearance of the garden.

The plants she grows, as well as passing the tests of taste and size, have to do well in the shade. The perennial herbs are mainly grown in pots so as to restrain their size and leave the deep soil of the beds for more demanding vegetables. The exception is a favourite, rosemary, which she can see from the house through the glass door. The pleasure she gets from it is worth the space it takes, though she does keep it well trimmed. Flowers are grown wherever there's room, and sweet peas join the climbing beans making use of the vertical space, which is always a valuable resource in such a small garden.

In front of the house is an even tinier patio, which faces directly south. It has a hot microclimate and Cristina regards it as her greenhouse. The ground is concrete and she grows almost everything there in pots: a fig, a bay tree, a few special herbs, some winter salads and a few flowers, some of which she will eventually plant out along the cycle path. There's also a grapevine. "I chose it for the colour of its autumn leaves," she says, "but this year it gave lovely sweet grapes." And that was despite the cold, rainy summer. It's in a planter made from drystone brick with a geo-fabric liner. This arrangement drains well – the concrete surface is slightly sloping – but soil doesn't come out of the bottom when it rains.

In such a moist, shady garden, slugs and snails definitely need attention. She has used the nematode treatment but it's costly and she finds beer traps are more effective. The local pub gives her stale beer if she goes in around four o'clock, when they set up the pumps, and sometimes she uses instant baking yeast, which works just as well. The traps are out all winter and emptied once a fortnight. This gets rid of the resident molluscs but some come in during the growing season and she deals with these by protecting individual plants. She cuts the bottom out of a plant pot and puts it in the ground round a young plant with a strip of copper or a smear of Vaseline round the rim. The Vaseline is rather high maintenance because it runs in hot weather and soil gets splashed up onto it in rain. When the slug season is past she leaves the rings in the ground and uses them to direct water economically to each plant.

"People think you need to buy a whole lot of stuff for gardening," Cristina says, "but you don't, either to construct the garden or to make it all work. Once you've got a trowel and a pair of secateurs all you need is a compost bin and a water butt." In fact the main input to her garden is simply the attention she gives it. Gardening on this scale is a very relaxed occupation, with no big jobs that take up a lot of your time. "I can nurture each plant as an individual," she says, "feed it or protect it as necessary. By any standards that's intensive, even with my motley chaos of vegetables, perennial herbs and flowers." The result shows in the amount of food she's able to produce from such a small and shady garden.

Patrick's Tips for Small Gardens

▷ Think in terms of volume rather than area: make full use of vertical space, i.e. walls and fences.

▷ Vegetables for vertical space include: runner and climbing French beans, tomatoes, old-fashioned tall pea varieties, climbing squash, etc.

▷ Almost all fruits can be trained up vertical spaces. Cane fruits, especially the hybrid berries, are a good choice for small gardens, but beware of over-vigorous varieties.

▷ Growing tree fruits against walls takes a bit more skilled pruning but the yield of fruit per area of ground space occupied can be very high.

▷ Light and shade is often an important factor in small gardens. Note the shady and sunny parts of your garden in morning, noon and night, both in spring and in summer so as to build up an overall picture.

▷ Painting a wall white can help make the garden lighter.

▷ Plants with larger leaves tend to do better in shade than plants with smaller leaves. Salad plants, including lettuce, rocket, land cress and Welsh onion, benefit from partial shade in summer as it will discourage them from bolting.

▷ Bush and cane fruits and cooking varieties of tree fruits can generally manage with half the day in full sun. Dessert varieties of tree fruits really need the whole day in sun.

▷ When choosing what to grow, go for plants which are: expensive to buy or hard to find in the shops, best eaten as fresh as possible, easy to grow or are the family's favourites. Don't waste precious space on things like potatoes and onions.

▷ Make raised beds. They can be any shape but the key feature is that every bit of bed can be reached from a path. No treading in the soil means no compaction and thus no need to dig.

Before

After

The south-facing, hot patio.

Abundance in a small space.

The Bunkhouse Garden

It was a pig of a design brief: the only work input to the garden would be a fortnight in spring, another in autumn and nine weeks in winter; these would also be the only times when produce could be harvested by the group (though other visitors could benefit at other times – but that wasn't the point!). All food growing had to be kept to the edges because most of the space was needed for other activities.

It was 1999. I'd been teaching permaculture and sustainable land use at Ragmans Lane Farm for three years, and thought it was about time we had a bit of practical permaculture going on in the piece of land right outside the accommodation and teaching building, the patch known as the bunkhouse garden.

Garden was perhaps a kind word for an area of rough grass containing a hot tub, a fire pit and some benches cut into the bank to make a little 'amphitheatre'. Two beds had been made against the wall of the main building but not yet planted up. The central grassy area was used for teaching and other activities, leaving only the one metre fence and a small patch adjacent to it as potential growing areas in addition to the beds.

The biggest limitation was not space but time. The farm staff kept the grass cut, but there was no-one who could take on looking after an extra bit of garden. So it had to be a garden that could survive and produce food just on the attention it would get while we were actually there running a course. During the growing season this amounted to two fortnights, one in June and the other in September. Of course this was when the food had to be ready to pick too.

Clearly annual vegetables were out. Only perennial vegetables and fruit were worth considering. Given the limitations of space, as well as the timing, I decided against top fruit. So it boiled down to soft fruit and perennial veg.

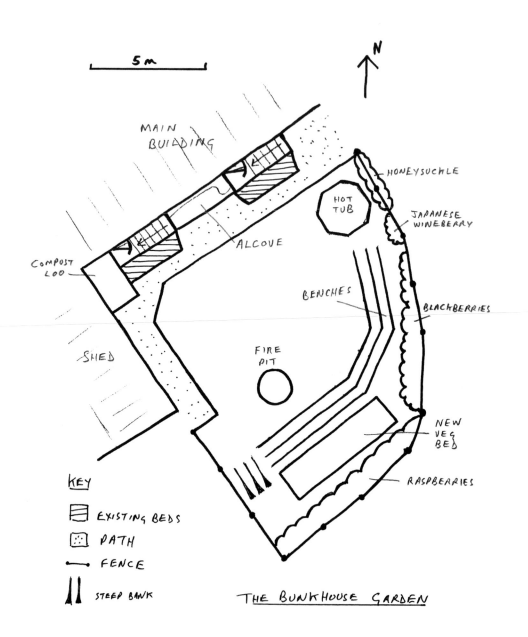

5 m

N

MAIN
BUILDING

HONEYSUCKLE

HOT
TUB

JAPANESE
WINEBERRY

ALCOVE

COMPOST
LOO

BENCHES

BLACKBERRIES

SHED

FIRE
PIT

NEW
VEG
BED

RASPBERRIES

KEY

EXISTING BEDS

PATH

FENCE

STEEP BANK

THE BUNKHOUSE GARDEN

September Soft Fruit

Choosing fruit that would be ripe in the first two weeks of September, not before or after, gave a whole new meaning to the word 'aim'. It's not just a matter of the odd gust of wind putting your row off course, but a whole season's weather possibly ripening your crop when there's no-one there to eat it.

There's one outdoor dessert grape, recommended for organic growing, which ripens in September. It's called Siegerrebe. I chose this to plant in the east of the two existing beds. The adjacent alcove, where we often sat with a cup of tea during a break and enjoyed the view of hills and woods, had a Perspex roof. So we trained the grape into the alcove. This not only gave it the perfect microclimate, but the Perspex protected it from rain and fungus diseases. It also meant we could reach up and help ourselves to bunches of delicious succulent grapes with a feeling of Roman decadence.

Perhaps the microclimate was too good, though. Two years in a row, the grapes ripened in August and the rotters on a course before ours had them!

My aim was better with the cane fruit. Along the southern border of the garden we planted two varieties of autumn fruiting raspberries, Autumn Bliss and Allgold. Allgold is a golden yellow raspberry with a delicious flavour which not only yields well in September but in some years has kept the farm people in raspberries right through to Christmas. Further along the fence we planted two September fruiting blackberries: Fantasia, which is vigorous and heavy cropping but with a flavour I personally find a bit sharp for eating raw, and Veronique, which is smaller and sweeter. Next I chose a Japanese wineberry, as much for its ornamental value as its fruit, which is usually too early for us. Finally, by the hot tub, we planted a native honeysuckle and a winter jasmine. The jasmine didn't survive the 'sink or swim' environment of this garden, but the honeysuckle thrived.

All the maintenance of the soft fruit was done during the winter Sustainable Land Use course. Pruning, weeding and mulching together made just one practical session for the students. During the September course, in the mornings before breakfast, foraging students converged on the bushes like bees round flowers, their bowls rapidly filling with multi-coloured berries. Fantasia also provided us with pie and pudding fillings.

Self-help Vegetables

I knew I could grow productive perennial vegetables with minimum of maintenance. That is what I do in my own garden at home. But how would they fare with long months without any attention at all?

In the existing beds by the building we planted Turkish rocket, herb patience and three kinds of perennial onions, together with nasturtiums as self-seeders.

The other place available for vegetables was between the raspberries and the top bench of the 'amphitheatre'. The soil here was deep and rich, but it was somewhat exposed to the prevailing south-west wind, the only shelter being provided by the fence immediately to the south-west.

Planting up one of the new beds in 2000.

The new bed, with cane fruit in the background, in 2002.

In March, at the end of the winter course, we mulched the ground with newspaper, edged the bed with slab wood and covered it with a 15cm (6in) layer of very old compost from a long-forgotten muck heap. Into this we put the plants I had raised in pots: sea beet, salad burnet, land cress, Welsh onion, Turkish rocket, musk mallow (from seed collected 50m/160ft away) and the pride and joy of perennial vegetables, Daubenton's perennial kale.

The sea beet found it too cold, and mostly died out the following winter. We planted more in the sheltered beds by the building, and now it gives us a good yield of greens for the June course. A fennel plant, which had self-seeded into a pot containing something else – I forget what – has become the mother and grandmother of several more fennels. Red deadnettle made its way into the bed and was a welcome addition to salads till it took its leave and departed. Apart from these, the general theme of this bed was a gradual dominance by the perennial kale.

There were two problems with not being there all the time. One was missing harvests. By the time you got there those lovely tender leaves had become a bit old and unappetising. The other was a direct consequence of this.

The vigorous plants grew all the bigger from not being harvested and tended to crowd out the less vigorous. These less vigorous ones hadn't disappeared, but the bulk of the biomass in the bed tended towards kale. This wouldn't have happened with sporadic harvesting through the growing season. But a gap from June to September left the field open to the strongest competitor.

Then, the autumn before last, while we weren't there, someone took down the fence that sheltered the bed. It was only a farm fence of pig netting, plain wire and a rail, but together with the nettle stalks which grew up around it made an effective windbreak. The kale took a real battering, and didn't yield much that year. It recovered by the end of the summer, and we put up a windbreak of woven willow. But the incident illustrates how, if you're not around, unexpected things can happen and have unforeseen consequences.

The maintenance requirement for the vegetables had been even less than for the fruit. A couple of people-hours of weeding and tidying up per year was all. The vigorous perennial vegetables left little space for weeds.

The Verdict

To sum up, the fruit was a great success and the vegetables well worthwhile. A key to the success of the fruit was that we were there in winter for pruning. An important factor for both fruit and veg was that the site was not deserted when we weren't there. Without the regular presence of people and the farm cat and dog I suspect most of the harvest would have been reaped by birds and rabbits.

Altogether I'm pleased with what we were able to grow with such a minimal input. In the next chapter we look at how to choose seed, the viability of seed saving, and how to sow seeds for the best results.

Swede and cabbage seedlings in modules.

7

Seeds

Choosing Vegetable Seeds at the Beginning of the Year

The wind may be howling, the rain may be sheeting down and the garden may look bare and bedraggled, but now is the time to think about buying seeds, before the rush starts.

The first step is to decide what you want to grow next year and see what seeds you have in stock. You may find that you don't have to buy very much. There's usually more than you need for one year's sowing in the average seed packet and if you've kept last year's surplus in a cool, dry place, out of direct light, there's no reason why you shouldn't use it this year. But do look at the best before date and take it seriously.

I'm ruthless about chucking out doubtful seed. There are many things that can go wrong after you sow seeds, so it's good if you can rest assured that at least the seed was OK. Otherwise, if the plants are late to emerge, it just adds to your doubts about whether you should re-sow.

For the same reason I'm a bit cautious about seeds swaps. They're lovely social occasions and I'm happy to take some of my home-saved seed and pick up some from other gardeners. But I have the same reluctance to sow other people's aged packets from the year before last or older as I have about my own, especially as I don't know how carefully they stored them.

What to Buy
The first question here is do you want to grow heritage varieties or modern ones? There are good reasons for both:
▷ Heritage varieties usually taste better.
▷ They're often more suitable for the home gardener than the commercial grower, e.g. peas which ripen little by little throughout the season rather than all at once for one big harvest.
▷ You may find something unusual, e.g. there are hundreds of varieties of tomato and lettuce that never make it to the mainstream catalogues.
▷ The people who grow and sell them are often the kind of small, ethical businesses that many of us want to support.
▷ Growing them helps keep genetic diversity where it belongs, in the fields and gardens rather than frozen in a gene bank.

On the other hand:
- ▷ Modern varieties usually have a higher yield.
- ▷ They may have been bred for resistance to specific diseases.
- ▷ You'll probably be more familiar with them and know exactly what you're going to get, which is an advantage if reliable crops are more important to you than experiment.

Should you use hybrids? Some people think that 'hybrid' means 'genetically modified'. It doesn't. It simply means that two strains of the same vegetable have been grown by inbreeding and then crossbred with each other to give the F1 generation, which is the seed you sow in your garden. The advantages of hybrids are that they often have qualities which other varieties lack and that final crossbreeding gives them extra vigour. The disadvantage is that you can't save your own seed from them, because it doesn't come true in the next generation. The choice is yours.

Where to Buy Them
See 'Resources' on page 131 for options.

Getting the Best Results from Spring Sown Annuals

It's nearly the end of March and I haven't sown a seed yet. I reckon that here in the south of England, early April is about right. I used to rush to get them in early so as to make the harvesting season longer. But over the years I've learnt that a more relaxed attitude often gives better results. Seeds sown too early, often in a warm spell, can suffer a check if a cold spell follows, and this check affects the plants' vigour throughout their life. Or they just struggle with generally low temperatures. Later sown seeds are much more likely to have reasonable temperatures throughout their early life and grow steadily.

Modules
I raise all my seedlings in modules. It's more work than sowing them directly into the ground but it gets the little plants off to a much better start. It means fewer losses to slugs, as they spend their most vulnerable time in the greenhouse, which I can keep slug-free. It also means fewer gaps in the crops, and where you re-sow into a gap you get a much smaller plant that never really catches up with its neighbours.

A variation on modules is rootrainers. Originally developed for trees, these are useful for deep-rooted plants like sweet corn and runner beans. I was introduced to this idea by Deano Martin, who kindly gave me my first set of rootrainers.

Brassica seedlings growing in trays.

Compost

The real expert gardeners say you can't beat peat-based compost. Moorland Gold is a brand of compost based on peat particles dredged from reservoirs, so using it doesn't contribute to the destruction of peat bogs. I've used it with success. But I have also used my own mix: 2 parts municipal compost, 2 parts of fertile topsoil and 1 part sharp sand – and I really can't say it performs any worse. It's much cheaper, too.

Municipal compost is made from the garden waste people take into the local recycling centre. It's low in nutrients, but that's just what little seeds need. For a potting mix, where more nutrients are needed, it can be replaced with sieved garden compost.

Watering

It's very easy to get this wrong, either too much or too little – and the weather makes a huge difference to the amount of water needed. Until the seeds germinate you need to keep the surface layer moist. But once they germinate I always water from below, i.e. I stand the modules in a tray of water so the compost can suck it up. This way you can be sure you get the water where it's needed, down at the bottom of the module where the roots grow. Keeping the surface relatively dry helps prevent damping off disease.

Everyone has their own recipe for raising seedlings, depending on what kind of gardener they are. I would describe myself as the no-frills, laid-back kind. It works for me.

Japanese wineberry (*Rubus phoenicolasius*) is easy to grow
and produces delicious, sweet berries.

8

Plants

Growing our own food is not only a satisfying and enjoyable thing to do, but it's also one of the most positive actions we can take to turn our negative ecological impact into a beneficial one.

Many of us have busy lives and small gardens, and lack the skills to provide a year-round supply of all the vegetables we would like to eat. If we can't grow everything we eat how do we decide which vegetables are most worth growing? Which ones give the best return on the time, energy and space we can devote to gardening?

They are likely to be those that are:

▷ Best eaten as fresh as possible
▷ Expensive to buy, or hard to find in the shops
▷ Easy to grow successfully
▷ Low in work requirement
▷ Heavy yielding
▷ Especially liked by the family.

Of course not many crops, if any, meet every one of these criteria, but any one that meets two or more is certainly worth considering. We all have somewhat different priorities. Someone who is new to gardening may put ease of growing first, while someone with a very small garden may put more emphasis on maximum yield, and so on.

Salads obviously qualify on the freshness count. There is an enormous variety of salad plants which can be grown in our climate, both annual and perennial, many of them attractive plants to look at.

Maincrop potatoes come at the other end of the scale, though some people may think the delight of extra-fresh new potatoes makes them worth the space.

Many of the salad plants which can be grown are hard to find in the shops, or expensive if they are available. Rocket and lamb's lettuce are examples, but they are both easy to grow at home. Garlic is expensive too, yet one of the easiest of crops to grow in my experience.

Ease of growing is something that varies from place to place, from season to season, and from gardener to gardener. Carrots, for example, are not that difficult to grow in a light or medium soil, but a real challenge on a heavy soil.

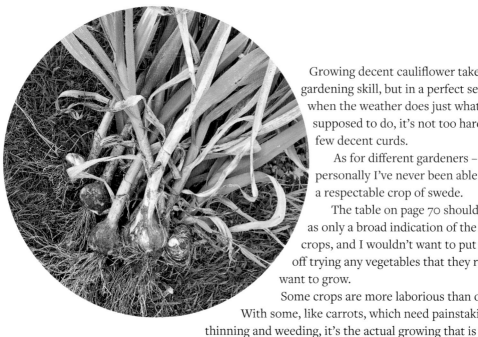

Growing decent cauliflower takes some gardening skill, but in a perfect season, when the weather does just what it's supposed to do, it's not too hard to get a few decent curds.

As for different gardeners – personally I've never been able to grow a respectable crop of swede.

The table on page 70 should be taken as only a broad indication of the easier crops, and I wouldn't want to put anyone off trying any vegetables that they really want to grow.

Some crops are more laborious than others. With some, like carrots, which need painstaking thinning and weeding, it's the actual growing that is laborious. But often it's the harvesting and preparation that really take time. I don't grow Brussels sprouts, for example, because I don't like the long fiddly jobs of preparing them for cooking.

Crops that must be planted in succession in order to get a continuous supply, like headed lettuce and spinach, take a lot of time to grow. Pick-and-pluck crops are much less time-consuming alternatives. With these vegetables you take repeated pickings over a long growing season rather than growing them to maturity then harvesting the whole plant. They include the loose-leaf varieties of lettuce and perpetual spinach or Swiss chard.

But the way the vegetables are grown has at least as much influence on the time taken as does the selection of crops. Doing away with the habit of digging makes a big difference. I've grown potatoes by the digging method and the mulch method and I would never go back to digging now. Weeding can take even more time than digging. Keeping the ground weed-free from the start and never letting annual weeds seed will save more work than anything else a gardener can do.

The crops that take least work of all to grow are the perennials, including fruits and perennial vegetables (see page 89).

Yields vary greatly according to soil, microclimate, seasoned grow. The yields given in the table (page 70) should be taken as a very rough guide to the sort of quantities you can expect from different crops. Even the relative yields will vary from year to year as each season will be better suited to some crops than others. But rough as they are, if you want to get the maximum out of a small area, they can suggest which crops to go for.

In larger gardens it is possible to over-produce and nothing is worse than seeing vegetables you have lovingly grown thrown on the compost heap. Having a rough idea of the produce you will get from a given area of a particular crop can help avoid this.

Crops that stay in the ground for a long time effectively have a low yield. Purple sprouting broccoli for example, delicious as it is, is in the ground for the best part of a year. A keen gardener could grow two crops, one summer and one winter, on that ground in the same time. But the yield could be increased by interplanting the broccoli with fast-growing crops, such as lettuce. Radishes, on the other hand, although small, grow quickly. They can be grown as a catch crop, fitted in before or after another crop, so their effective yield can be as high as that from larger roots.

The luxury perennials, asparagus and globe artichoke, not only have a low yield but are in the ground for 18 months to two years before they start producing. But if taste and expense are your criteria they are certainly worth growing.

Continuity of supply can be as important as the total yield. In a very small garden you are likely to eat everything you grow, and expect to supplement what you grow with bought vegetables. But with larger gardens it's all too easy to have a glut of vegetables at any one time followed by a shortage a few weeks later. In fact, achieving perfect continuity of supply is one of the greatest skills of gardening. The problem is greatest with successional crops like radish, spinach and headed lettuce, giving another reason for growing the pick-and-pluck alternatives.

With crops that are harvested all at once, or over a short season, careful storage is the key to continuity of supply. Vegetables that can be stored without freezing or bottling include potatoes, roots, the pumpkin family, white cabbage, onions, garlic and even tomatoes. This does take some care and attention, and suitable storage space.

A bountiful summer harvest.

The mythical 'well-ventilated, cool, frost-free shed' is ideal. If you have doubts about storing vegetables successfully it may be wise to limit the amount of these crops you grow, even in a large garden.

Almost every home garden has its herbs. They qualify for inclusion on the freshness count, and the perennial ones (most of them) are easy to grow with low work requirement. But they are one of the easiest things to grow too much of. A single sage or rosemary plant can in three or four years grow to a size that would keep a small village supplied. In small gardens where maximum production is an aim, these herbs must be kept regularly pruned.

It comes hard to many people to cut and discard something that is potentially edible, and it may be possible to dry the leaves and sell them or give them away. But an unused potential is not a useful yield, and it's more productive to compost unwanted herb leaves and grow something else in the liberated space. It can be worthwhile to allow the plants to grow big deliberately for their visual effect. But so often they simply grow because we forget to prune them.

What the family likes to eat is to some extent the factor that must be balanced with all the others put together. If there's nothing on Earth you like more than globe artichokes, don't worry about the low yield and the fact that it's not the easiest plant to grow!

Allotments

The criteria for choosing what crops to grow on an allotment are quite different from those that apply to a small home garden. Most allotment holders only get to visit their

Potatoes, garlic and lettuces growing on an allotment patch.

Brainse Ráth Maonais
Rathmines Branch
Fón / Tel: 4973539

plot once a week, whereas you can potter in your back garden every evening in spring and summer. Crops that need work in large but infrequent doses, and which will keep for a week or more after picking, are best for allotments. Potatoes, onions, cabbage and roots are obvious choices, especially if they are maincrops for winter storage. If your local allotment rules allow it, and scrumping is not too much of a problem, planting fruit can also be a good choice. (Editor's note: scrumping is an English term for stealing fruit.)

Obviously a family who only have an allotment will have to grow their whole range of crops there, but it may be a narrower range than they would grow if they had a patch of land right outside the kitchen window. For those who have both, a garden and an allotment can complement each other well.

Finally, whatever selection of vegetables we would like to grow, we have to fit them into a rotation. If too many of the chosen plants are closely related it may be difficult to create enough of a break between them to avoid problems of pest and disease build-up in the soil. If that's the case it may be necessary to adjust the selection somewhat. This is what I have had to do in my own garden.

Three families of vegetables are especially prone to soil-borne pests and diseases:

▷ the brassicas,
▷ the onion family,
▷ and the potato/tomato family.

These should never be grown more than once in four years on the same soil. Although other families are less troubled by soil-borne maladies, all vegetables are best grown on rotation. There are good books on organic gardening that give the framework

within which you can fit the crops you want to grow to give a balanced and healthy rotation.

My Own Selection

The largest part of our garden is planted with fruit and perennial vegetables, which provide us with all our salads and most of our greens. But we also have a small plot of annuals where we grow:

▷ Broad beans, autumn sown – very easy to grow, and we love them.

▷ Garlic – easy to grow, expensive to buy, and we have a variety with very large cloves, which saves a lot of work in the kitchen compared to the garlic you can buy.

▷ Leeks – a reliable and heavy-yielding crop that we eat frequently in winter.

▷ Squash – not the easiest thing to grow in our slug-infested garden, but we eat a lot of it, and once it gets going it's a good weed smothering crop.

▷ Swiss chard – although we have it self-seeding in the perennial garden, we can never get too much of it, and it gives a fourth course to the rotation; easy to grow and yields well.

▷ Winter radish – fills a gap in the rotation, and makes a spicy addition to winter salads.

Lettuce, garlic and carrots on the allotment

Garden potatoes mid-season.   The same patch after harvest.

Rotation

The need to rotate the onion family means we don't fit in as many leeks as we would like. But we usually find a spare corner in the perennial garden for a few extra. The other annual vegetable we grow is sweet corn. It's low yielding, but we love it and it really does need to be eaten immediately after picking. This fits in here and there in the perennial garden as an upper storey above lower-growing things. It usually does very well like that, and the combined yield of the double-storey crop is quite respectable.

This is a very simple example, but the principles are just the same if you have the time and space to grow a much wider range of vegetables.

	Yield	Easy to Grow?	Amount of Work	Notes
Some Common Vegetables Compared				
Potatoes, maincrop	M	E	3	
Potatoes, early	L	E	3	
Jerusalem artichokes	M	E	1	best as perennial
Peas, dwarf	L	D	3	
Beans, broad	L	E	1	
Beans, dwarf French	L	M	2	
Beans, runner	H	M	3	
Carrots	H	M	3	difficult on heavy soil
Radishes, summer	L	E	1	
Radishes, winter	M	E	1	
Parsnips	M	M	1	
Beetroot	M	M	1	+ tops
Turnips	L	M	1	+ tops
Swedes	H	M	1	heaviest yield of all
Broccoli, calabrese and purple sprouting	L	D	2	
Cauliflower	L	D	2	
Brussels sprouts	L	M	3	
Kale, annual	L	E	2	
Kale, perennial	M	E	1	
Cabbage	M	E	2	
Swiss chard and perpetual spinach	M	E	1	self-seeders
Spinach	L	D	3	
Garlic	L	E	1	
Onions	M	M	2	
Leeks	H	E	2	

Lettuce, hearted	L	M	2	
Lettuce, loose leaf	H	M	2	
Pumpkin	L	E	1	
Squash	L	E	1	
Courgettes	H	E	1	
Sweet corn	VL	M	3	4 cobs/m²
Tomatoes, outdoor	M	M	3	
Asparagus	VL	D	2	60-75 spears/m²
Globe artichokes	VL	D	2	10-12 heads/m²

Key
Yield:
H = Heavy, more than 5kg/m²
M = Moderate, around 5kg/m²
L = Light, around 2.5kg/m²
VL = Very light, 1kg/m² or less

Easy to Grow?:
E = Easy
M = Moderate
D = Difficult

Amount of Work:
1 = Light
2 = Moderate
3 = Heavy

Mizuna and rocket grown in a raised planter to avoid slug damage.

9

Slugs

When we moved into this hamlet, one of our new neighbours said, "The only way to grow any vegetables here is to have a large tub of slug pellets and use them constantly." After our first year's gardening I could see her point. Even for the wet west of Britain, the spot is unusually sluggy.

Our second season in the west was a notoriously bad slug year over most of the country, so you can imagine what it was like here. Our garden produced little food. Its main yield being knowledge about how to co-exist with slugs.

Of course, there are chemical, mechanical and biological methods of control, some of which we have tried in our garden. But we have also learned a good deal about how to avoid competing with slugs, by choosing the vegetables they least like to eat, and growing others in a way that avoids slug attack. So let's look at the different forms of slug control available to the permaculturist.

Chemical Control

The use of aluminium sulphate was occasionally accepted by the Soil Association but they have now decided it isn't sustainable in the full sense, because adding a poisonous heavy metal to the soil over hundreds of years, even in tiny quantities, will eventually lead to toxicity. Any truly sustainable practice must be safe to use indefinitely. Aluminium sulphate's advantage is that it doesn't kill anything other than slugs and snails. Its disadvantage is that it doesn't actually kill them very effectively. It can have a marginal effect on a mild slug problem, but that's about all.

The Soil Association has also allowed organic growers to use metaldehyde slug pellets in extreme cases, though only round the edges of fields, where slugs have the nearby cover of the hedgebottom. The problem with metaldehyde is that it's poisonous to mammals and birds as well as molluscs, and they can die, either by eating the pellets or by eating slugs which have eaten them. They are poisonous to the carabid beetle as well which also preys on slugs.

As our neighbour suggested, in a home garden in a really bad slug year, pellets are only effective if used overall, and constantly throughout the season. A friend of mine grew good crop by totally surrounding his vegetable bed with a belt of pellets hidden under planks to keep them from the other creatures. You also need to dispose of dead slugs daily. But personally I haven't the stomach for such intensive reliance on poisons.

Mechanical Control

The conventional organic answer to slugs is to grow vegetables in as large a block as possible, with no plants present other than the crop, no mulch, and the maximum of cultivation. This minimises the places where slugs can hide within striking distance of the crop plants, and the cultivation exposes the slugs' eggs, which are laid in the soil, to birds and other predators. This is effective. Our local organic market garden, where most of the vegetables are grown in a single large field, has no slug problem. But it could hardly be further from the rich ecosystem of the ideal permaculture garden: lots of mulch and ground cover plants, minimal cultivations, and an intimate mixture of trees, shrubs, perennials and annuals. It's also not really an option for the small home garden, where you are never far from a slug haven, even in the middle of the vegetable patch.

The most effective slug trap in terms of input of human effort per slugs killed is a plank, or any other flat object, laid on the soil. During the day the slugs hide under it to escape the comparatively dry daytime conditions, and you can scoop them up in large quantities. Of course, if you leave the planks down and then don't come you're just giving them an extra shelter right beside your vegetables. Picking slugs off the vegetables at dusk or during rain can help young plants survive a moderate slug population or mature plants a heavy population. But a single slug can kill a little cabbage plant – you only have to miss one.

Barrier Methods

Mulches of dry or prickly substances round the plants, such as wood ash, sawdust or dry oak leaves, are a waste of time. They only form an effective barrier to slugs when they are dry. As soon as it rains – which is when the slugs come out – they are useless.

Plastic collars, made by cutting the ends off mineral water bottles, placing them round newly planted-out seedlings and pressing them well into the ground, make a more effective barrier. They improve the chance of the seedlings growing through their most vulnerable stage, and can make a big difference in a moderate slug infestation. But slugs do sometimes get inside them and, in a bad season, when the plants are growing slowly anyway due to cool, wet weather, losses can still be very high.

The best barrier method is a conservatory, greenhouse, polytunnel, cold frame or cloche. In these enclosed spaces it is possible to maintain a relatively dry micro-climate, and though slugs do get in, they will be few enough to control easily by hand-picking as soon as you see any damage.

Plants are at their most vulnerable when small. Sowing seeds of most vegetables directly in the ground is pointless if slugs are abundant, so plants must be raised under cover and planted out. A small cold frame, which can be made from windows rescued from skips, or bought for less than £20, is enough space to raise plants for a moderate sized vegetable plot. We have one raised up on an old table to make it more difficult for the slugs to find their way in.

Biological Control

The ideal solution to an excess of slugs is to introduce a predator, such as ducks or frogs – both of which also eat snails. This avoids both the dangers of mucking about with poisons and the extra work involved in mechanical methods.

Ducks are very effective. They need to be managed carefully; only let them into the garden when there are slugs to be eaten and take them out when they have finished them and want to start on the vegetables. Some plants, like strawberries, will need to be netted to keep them off. It's also important to choose the right breed: Khaki Campbells and Indian Runners are the best, because they are the most carnivorous breeds. You also need to have the necessary commitment to looking after animals, and enough space to keep them properly when they're not on slug duty in the vegetable plot.

A high population of frogs will keep the slug population within bounds, though it takes a year or two for the frogs to get big enough to eat slugs. A pond is necessary for frogs to breed in. It can be tiny, say a metre across, and can be allowed to dry up in late summer after the tadpoles have become frogs. The adult frogs need dense, low vegetation to live in the rest of the year – in fact just the kind of thing slugs love to hide up in! You can wait for frogs to discover your pond and breed in it, or, to make sure, collect some frog spawn in early spring and put that in.

Slug-resistant Plants

I have made and stocked a little frog pond, but the question remains what to grow in the year or two before the frogs are big enough. This year has taught me some answers. The overall principle is to avoid conflict with the slugs, and there are five main ways of doing this:
1) Don't grow the plants they most like to eat.
2) Grow things that are at their young, vulnerable stage when the slugs are least active.
3) Plant seedlings rather than sowing seed.
4) Grow perennial vegetables, which are only in the vulnerable seedling stage once in their lifetime.
5) Grow native plants, which have much more natural resistance than our regular garden plants, which are all either introductions or have been artificially bred for so long as to have lost their inborn resistance.

Here are a few suggestions for the different classes of garden vegetables.

Salads

Forget about growing lettuces if slugs are a real problem. The red-leaved ones are more resistant than the green, and may survive a mild infestation, especially if protected with plastic collars when planted out. Endives seem to be immune to slugs, and can substitute for lettuce. But they are rather bitter, and need to be blanched by excluding light, which is usually done by placing a dinner plate or something similar over the mature plant. The slugs love to shelter under these plates, but strangely don't seem to demolish the endives as soon as they are fit to eat. You have to be quick, though.

Lamb's lettuce and land cress are hardly touched by slugs. Watercress, which can be grown in any moist soil, not just in water, is a perennial, but it is less resistant to slugs and difficult to establish when there are many of them about. The best way is to plant some of the sprigs you buy from the greengrocer rather than trying to sow seed.

Another perennial is salad burnet, a great salad stand-by all year round. It is a native plant, just one of many listed by Richard Mabey in his wonderful book, *Food for Free* – essential reading for the permaculture gardener. Chickweed is another native, a self-seeding annual, a fine substitute for lettuce.

Greens

If you are determined to grow the cabbage family, it can be worthwhile to persist with planting out seedlings in plastic collars. But if the slug infestation is bad you may only end up with a few plants, despite frequent replanting.

Spring cabbage avoids the slug problem because it's planted out in October, when slugs are much less active than in June, when the other brassicas are planted. I extend the picking season by planting close together, taking every other plant for spring greens, letting the others grow on for hearted cabbage, and after harvesting these, leaving the stems in the ground to sprout again for a later crop. If you cut a cross in the top of the stem four little cabbages will sprout from it. This way the autumn planting can be made to last a good part of the year.

Nine star broccoli is a perennial, so it is more worthwhile investing energy in getting some of this established, because you will get about five years, cropping for your trouble.

Good King Henry is a perennial spinach. It can be started off in pots and planted out in the autumn.

Chinese greens – pak choi and the like – are particularly susceptible to slugs.

Root crops

The only root vegetable that is not grown from seed each year is the perennial skirret. It has a many forked root, and one branch of this can be returned to the soil after lifting to regrow for next year. But perennials grown from seed in the open ground are just as susceptible to slugs in their first year as are annuals, so it may be necessary to start skirret off under cover in the first year and plant the roots out in autumn

The Marrow Family

Squashes, pumpkins, marrows and courgettes are as difficult to grow in a really bad slug year as the summer-planted cabbages. But if you start off with many more plants than you need, to allow for heavy losses, you can get a crop of sorts in the worst of times.

Beans

I don't think runner beans are worth the effort. Despite our best efforts, we've struggled with runner beans. The same goes for French beans. Broad beans, on the other hand, can get away with minimal losses, especially if they are autumn sown. I haven't tried English field beans, but I expect they are slug-hardy too.

Onion

Garlic appears to be totally immune to slugs. I haven't tried maincrop onions in this garden, but I see no reason why onion sets and shallots shouldn't do well in the face of slugs. Spring onions grown from seed didn't stand a chance, but the perennial Welsh onions proved to be an excellent substitute, providing plenty of leaves for salad throughout the year.

Sweet corn

This did well when raised in the cold frame and planted out with plastic collars.

This list is certainly not comprehensive, and what is true in one garden in one season is not necessarily true in another time and place. But I hope my experience will give some idea of where to start to those who want to grow some of their own food in a slug-infested garden without having to cover the soil with poisonous pellets.

A minimalist garden with an ornamental twist.

10

Plants for the Minimalist Garden

Here Patrick provides his selection for those plants that best suit a minimalist garden. These include sea beet, ramsons, perennial kale, Welsh onions, pink purslane and perennial salads.

Ramsons (*Allium ursinum*)

A woodland perennial, found all over Britain, ramsons (wild garlic) is a real shade lover. It rarely does well in full sun, but given shade from deciduous trees and a moist, alkaline soil it can outcompete most other herbaceous plants.

It is the broad-bladed leaves that are eaten, not the bulbs, which are tiny. It is ready to pick in March and dies down again in June. This makes it a good complement to bulb garlic, arriving when last year's dried bulbs are often running out, and just when the first green bulbs of this year's crop are ready. It is also excellent in salads, or as a sandwich filling with cottage cheese or peanut butter. The flowers, brilliant white globes, brighten up the shady parts of the garden in May. Seed can be bought from wildflower suppliers. The plants can be raised in pots and planted out during the dormant season or seed can be sown direct. A spacing of 10cm is about right.

Sea Beet
(*Beta vulgaris* ssp. *maritima*)

A wild perennial that grows around the coast of England and Wales, this is the ancestor of beetroot, chard and other cultivated beets (which have all had the perenn-ialism bred out of them). It is an excellent spinach, with a taste as good as, if not better than, cultivated kinds. Unlike many edible wild plants the leaves are large, so picking is quick and easy. The picking season is from April to October in cooler areas, and all year round in milder areas, though winter picking should be very light. Peak production is in May and June, tailing off after flowering, when the leaves get smaller.

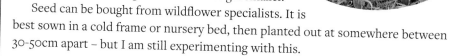

Seed can be bought from wildflower specialists. It is best sown in a cold frame or nursery bed, then planted out at somewhere between 30-50cm apart – but I am still experimenting with this.

Perennial Kale (*Brassica oleracea*)

Like the beets, all the garden brassicas are descended from a wild seaside perennial, but perennial kale is the only true perennial among them.[†] It is tough, multi-stemmed, clump-forming and virtually immortal. Although it can play host to the common pests of brassicas, it is relatively unaffected by them.

It is green throughout the year, and starts growth early in the spring. The leaves are often rather small, about the size of well-grown common spinach, and have a nutty taste that is much better than the annual varieties of kale.

Stem cuttings will take any time from spring to autumn, and should be planted at around 60cm apart. In a year or two they will grow to form a thick clump, and although it will spread, it is not invasive.

[†] Nine Star perennial broccoli is monocarpic, i.e. it lives for a few years but dies immediately if allowed to set seed, and it cannot reproduce vegetatively.

Welsh Onions (*Allium fistulosum*)

These are a tough, perennial alternative to spring onions, growing in dense clumps up to 50cm tall. They stay green all winter in mild areas. The red-bulbed varieties are hardier than more common white-bulbed ones.

The plants should be renewed every few years to keep them healthy. They often self-seed, but if they don't, a few plants can be detached from the outside of the clump and replanted elsewhere, at 20cm apart. The leaves regrow vigorously after picking and can be harvested intensively. The bulbs can be picked as well, but they regrow much more slowly, and you will get more from the plants if you only take the leaves. Although their main use is in salads they can be used for cooking if no other onions are available.

Everlasting onions (*A. perutile*) are similar, smaller plants that stay green all winter in colder areas. They do not self-seed.

Pink Purslane (*Montia sibirica*)

I have seen this little plant carpeting the ground in dense woodland high on Dartmoor, often on very wet soils, so it is an obvious choice for gardens that are shady, poorly drained, acid or cold. But it is not confined to these conditions, and should do well anywhere that is reasonably moist, though the flavour is better in cool weather and a shady situation.

The leaves can be used in salads or cooked, and have a mild flavour with a hint of spinach or beetroot. The small pale pink flowers do not make a striking display, but add some extra colour to the garden in spring and early summer.

It is an annual, or short-lived perennial, and self-seeds readily. If it comes up thickly it can be used for cut-and-come again, or thinned to about 20cm apart. It only grows to 25cm or less, and can be used as a ground cover between or below taller plants.

Perennial Salad Plants

Turkish rocket (*Bunias orientalis*) is not a perennial substitute for the better-known annual rocket, as the taste is quite different. Turkish rocket has a fairly hot, fresh taste without the nuttiness of its annual namesake. The leaves are at their best when young, and if they grow large are best picked and used as mulch, to encourage the young ones to grow.

It has pickable leaves as early as March in a mild spring, but this year in my garden in Somerset, we couldn't pick any until May. It can stand a good deal of neglect and competes well with weeds. Plants should be spaced about 50cm apart.

French scorzonera (*Reichardia picroides*) is a smaller, more delicate plant. It's a member of the dandelion family, but the taste could hardly be more different. Where dandelions are sour, 'Richard' – as I call it – is mild and sweet and makes a good substitute for lettuce. Unfortunately it is not very hardy and can be killed off in a cold winter, but it can self-seed freely, and is resistant to slugs. A spacing of 20-25cm should be adequate.

Turkish rocket.

French scorzonera.

Cut-and-Come-Again

This is like the mustard and cress we used to grow in the airing cupboard as children. The seedlings are not thinned, but cut overall with scissors when they reach about 3-7cm high. This can be repeated anything from 2-5 times, depending on the kind of plants, time of year and weather conditions. It is generally more successful in spring and autumn than in high summer, when the weather is drier and the plants tend to go to seed. A patch first cut in the autumn can sometimes overwinter and be cut again in spring.

It is one of the most productive ways to grow leafy vegetables, as they cover the ground completely almost from the start and grow fast. The nutritional value of the seedlings is also higher than that of older plants – they can have twice the vitamin content.

Self-Seeders

Cut-and-come again salad leaves.

Lamb's lettuce, also known as corn salad, is a mild tasting salad plant, low-growing with a small rosette of round-shaped leaves. It can be substituted for lettuce in a salad. It is very much a plant of the winter and spring, not germinating until autumn and going to seed in spring. It self-seeds so prolifically that it can sometimes be used as a winter green manure.

Land cress and rocket are stronger tasting than lamb's lettuce, with rocket having a delicious nutty taste. They also prefer the cool of autumn and spring, though they can be kept going into the summer by picking the flowers as they form and keeping the soil moist, but the taste becomes increasingly hotter. Rocket can be killed by a hard frost, but lamb's lettuce and land cress are extremely frost hardy.

These three plants grow well together, and go well together in a salad. They also look very pretty together when all three are in flower: the bright yellow of the cress contrasting with the marbled white of the rocket and the sky blue of the lamb's lettuce. Seed can be bought in any good garden shop. (See page 101 for more on salads.)

Three 'Real Weeds'

Chickweed is another lettuce substitute, with a pleasant mild taste. It does well in part shade and is extremely cold hardy – you can scrape away the snow and find excellent chickweed beneath.

Fat hen can be added to a salad or cooked on its own like spinach, for one minute. It is delicious either way, especially when young, with a savoury, slightly salty taste. (Though, like common spinach, it is high in oxalic acid, so should not be eaten every day.)

Hairy bittercress is not noticeably hairy and not at all bitter. It is in fact the best tasting of all the cress, nutty, with just a hint of pepper. It is a very small plant, and its contribution to a salad is one of taste rather than bulk. It grows best in moist, shady places.

If these plants turn up in your garden, don't weed them out harvest them! I have even introduced them, but beware, they will rapidly colonise any bare ground.

Three Edible Flowers

Nasturtiums are a brilliant edible/ornamental plant. Leaves, stems, the brightly coloured flowers and the seed pods can all be used in salads. The taste is peppery but mild. The trailing varieties can cover large areas of ground quickly, and climb up fences etc. They are not the most reliable of self-seeders, but probably worth hand-raising now and then to keep them going.

Pot marigolds come up much more reliably, often so thickly that they need thinning to get healthy plants that bloom well. Planting 20-25cm apart is about right. The bright orange flowers bring life to the garden, attract beneficial insects, and are edible, adding colour, taste and perhaps a health-giving ingredient to salads.

Many members of the viola family have edible flowers, from the tiny sweet violets to the large garden pansy. Perhaps the most useful one is the wild pansy or heartsease, a short-lived perennial whose natural home is grassland.

Land cress.

Mizuna.

Rocket.

Chickweed.

Hairy bittercress.

Fat hen.

Some Vegetables for a Minimalist Garden			
Name	Perennial or Self-seeder	Size: Low / Med / Tall	Main Use
Perennial kale (*Brassica oleracea*)	P	M	Greens
Nine star broccoli (*Brassica oleracea*)	P	T	Curds
Sea beet* (*Beta vulgaris* ssp. *maritima*)	P	M	Greens
Chard (*Beta vulgaris* ssp. *cicla*)	S	M	Greens
Good King Henry (*Chenopodium bonus-henricus*)	P	M	Greens
Fat hen* (*Chenopodium album*)	S	M	Greens
Sea kale (*Crambe maritima*)	P	M	Stems
Lovage (*Levisticum officinale*)	P	T	Stems
Alexanders (*Smyrnium olustratum*)	S	T	Stems
French scorzonera (*Reichardia picroides*)	P	L	Salad, mild
Pink purslane (*Montia sibirica*)	P&S	L	Salad, mild
Salad Burnet (*Sanguisorba minor*)	P&S	L/M	Salad, mild
Chickweed* (*Stellaria media*)	S	L	Salad, mild
Lamb's lettuce (*Valerianella locust*)	S	L	Salad, mild
Winter purslane (*Claytonia perfoliata*)	S	L	Salad, mild
Turkish rocket (*Bunias orientalis*)	P	M	Salad, tasty
Chicory (*Cichorium intybus*)	P	Various	Salad, tasty
Sorrel (*Rumex* spp.)	P	L/M	Salad, tasty
Land cress (*Barbarea verna*)	S	L/M	Salad, tasty
Rocket (*Eruca sativa*)	S	L/M	Salad, tasty
Hairy bittercress* (*Cardamine hirsuta*)	S	L	Salad, tasty
Nasturtium (*Tropaeolum majus*)	S	L	Salad, tasty
Ramsons* (*Allium ursinum*)	P	L/M	Leaves
Welsh onions (*Allium. fistulosum*)	P	M	Leaves
Everlasting onions (*Allium. perutile*)	P	L	Leaves
Tree onions (*Allium. cepa proliferum*)	P	M	Bulbs
Skirret (*Sium sisarum*)	P	M	Roots

Notes
Sizes are approximate only:
Low – less than 30cm;
Medium – 30-60cm;
Tall – over 60cm.

*   Indicates a wild plant – seed available from wildflower specialists. Many seed
     catalogues list perennial vegetables under 'Herbs'.

Marigolds grown in a pot.

Viola.   Nasturtium.

Jersey walking kale.

11

Patrick's Favourite Perennial Vegetables

When I first got into permaculture 20 years ago, I was intrigued by the idea of perennial vegetables. Quite soon I decided to make them the mainstay of my garden. My aim was to see just how feasible it is to make a garden that acts like a self-regulating ecosystem, with minimum need for maintenance. After good soil preparation and careful propagation, I more or less left the plants to get on with it. Many fell by the wayside. In particular anything that was susceptible to slugs died out. I would protect plants through the seedling stage, when almost any plant is vulnerable to slugs, but after that it was sink or swim. Sea kale never stood a chance. Things that I don't like the taste of also got the chop. So goodbye to Good King Henry and Babbington's leek.

Then in 2009 I decided to change the whole emphasis of my gardening from low maintenance to high yield. This meant changing from mainly perennials with a few easy-to-grow annuals to mainly annuals plus a few perennials that have stood the test of time. I don't mean to say that annuals are intrinsically higher-yielding than perennials. They're not. But you do end up eating more of what you grow in an annual garden because there's a much wider range of annual vegetables than perennials. Perennials are mainly leafy greens and salads. Your garden may be bursting with perennial kale, but if you've already had it twice that week you will probably find yourself going out and buying carrots or green beans.

This change put a sharp selection pressure on my perennials. With 20 years of experience behind me, these are the ones I've kept:

Daubenton's Perennial Kale

It grows from cuttings, hardly ever flowers and is one of the most resistant edible plants I know. It gets affected by cabbage whites, mildew and so on but, though you might lose a few weeks' production, the plant just shrugs them off and grows again, where an annual would turn up its heels and die. It provides tasty leaves all the year round. Pick them by the handful; they're too small to pick one by one. One plant can easily spread to a metre wide in its second year.

I also started growing Jersey walking stick kale, which has a different taste to Daubentons, which is useful (see page 88).

Sea Beet

This is the perennial form of Swiss chard or leaf beet. These two are brilliant self-seeders if you allow one plant to grow on into its second year, when it flowers and sets seed. So why bother with the perennial kind? Well, it has a richer, stronger taste, which is excellent for soups, and it's at its most productive in May, the hungry gap in the annual garden. Allow half a metre of space for it and cut it back if it straggles further than that. (See page 80.)

Herb Patience
(*Rumex patiencia*)

A larger-leaved, milder-tasting version
of sorrel, it can be used in large
quantities in salads and makes a good
soup with a lemony tang when mixed
with sea beet, along with a little onion,
garlic and potato. It comes up early in
spring, dies right down in midsummer
and comes up again in late summer.
The flowering head is taller than me but
it only needs some 30cm of horizontal
space.

Musk Mallow
(*Malva moschata*)

A native wildflower with white or pink
flowers, it produces lots of small, mild
tasting leaves that you can harvest by
the handful in spring. When it flowers,
the leaves become more widely spaced
and less easy to harvest. You can then
either pick the flowers, which are also
edible, or rejuvenate the plant by
cutting it down to the ground so it
grows back in its leafy, springtime
form. It makes a good base for a salad,
to which you can add tastier leaves.
Allow 25cm per plant.

Onions (*Allium* spp.)

There are probably more perennial onions than all other perennial vegetables put together. They're mainly used in salads, as the cookable parts tend to be a bit on the small side compared with annual onions.

First to come in spring is wild garlic or ramsons (*A. ursinum*), which will carpet the ground in the shadiest part of your garden. Harvest the leaves and they'll give the same 'je ne sais quoi' to a salad that bulb garlic gives to a cooked dish. They die down in early summer but you can enjoy the garlic flavour in salads by switching to garlic chives (*A. tuberosum*), which produce leaves all summer. Allow 10-15cm per plant for garlic chives.

Welsh onions (*A. fistulosum*) (see page 81) and tree onions (*A. cepa viviparum*) are both like large versions of common chives, needing about 20cm per plant. The leaves are excellent in salads. Welsh onions do better in partial shade as it keeps the leaves fresh and juicy and makes the plants reluctant to go to flower, when the leaves become fibrous and inedible for a while. The two kinds complement each other because they flower at different times, so the supply of fresh green leaves is not interrupted. Strictly speaking the tree onion doesn't flower. It produces little bulbils instead which you can use to propagate it.

Minogue onion is known to me by that name because the gardener I got it from had it from her uncle Fred, whose surname was Minogue. A student of mine from New Zealand recognised it as what they call miners' weed down there, because it spreads so much, but I can't say it's been a problem in my garden. I don't know what its botanical name is but in structure it's more like garlic and leeks than onions, with a bladed leaf

Tree onion.

rather than a round one. In winter it makes a big clump of strong-tasting salad onions. The way to harvest it is to dig up the clump, detach as many bulbs as you want and replant. In summer it dies right down below ground and forms round bulbs a couple of centimetres across. You can use these for cooking and they're not too fiddly to prepare because they don't need peeling. Plant about 20cm apart.

Others

One plant I must mention, though not a vegetable, is the Alpine strawberry. Unlike the wild strawberry it doesn't spread by suckers so it's not invasive. It fruits from early summer right through to October and though the fruits rarely amount to enough to fill a bowl they make a wonderful snack while you're gardening.

Self-seeders I would never be without are: lamb's lettuce, land cress, winter purslane and rocket (see page 83). These are all salads and are mainly autumn to spring yielders. In my garden, rocket only self-seeds in the greenhouse but the others do well outside. Incidentally, when I changed the garden from perennial to annual I discovered something about self-seeders: they love digging. Of course the perennial garden was never dug and I intend to make the annual garden no-dig as well. But I took the opportunity of the changeover to reorganise the beds and dig in compost and rock dust. The self-seeders came up in quantities I'd never seen before, carpeting the ground so closely you couldn't see the soil. There was far too much to eat but they made a brilliant overwintering green manure, much better than the one I'd intentionally sown.

Another self-seeder, this time a summer one, is nasturtium. Both leaves and flowers are edible and once you've sown it you'll never need to sow it again. It also adds a dash of colour to the edible garden (see page 84).

Finally there are the herbs. I use mint, marjoram, lemon balm and fennel in salads only slightly less liberally than the stronger tasting salad vegetables, such as chicory. They say chicory's a perennial, by the way, but I've never been able to get it to live for more than one year. Has anyone else had better luck?

Alpine strawberry.

Oregano, closely related to marjoram.

Squash, sweet corn, courgette and bean polyculture.

12

Polycultures

D iversity is one of the principles of permaculture. Following the model of natural ecosystems, we shy away from monocultures and like to mix our crops. This can be done intuitively, mixing vegetables, herbs, flowers and fruits almost at random. The resulting garden will probably be very healthy. Any pest or disease will find it hard to spread to problem proportions in a garden where every other plant is something it can't eat or infect. But the yield may not be very high.

If we design our mixtures carefully, however, we can actually get higher yields than we would by growing the same range of crops as monocultures. There are two main ways of doing this. The first is by choosing combinations that share resources rather than competing for them. The second is by combining one crop with another one that actually helps it.

Sharing Light

One of the best ways of avoiding competition between two crops is to put together one tall thin one and one short bushy one, such as sweet corn and squash. The corn is too thin to seriously shade the squash and the squash is too short to seriously shade the corn. Thus they share the resource of light rather than competing with each other for it. This means they're making fuller use of the incoming solar radiation, so the yield is potentially higher than it could be with a monoculture of either crop on its own.

Of course, light is not the only resource they both need. Water and mineral nutrients are others. These are the below ground resources, and there's not as much difference in the root shapes of corn and squash as there is above ground, so here they compete more. Thus to get full advantage from this combination you may need to water more, and will almost certainly need to apply more manure or compost. Still, it's worth it if a high yield per square metre is important to you, and an added bonus is that the squash will suppress weeds, and save you that job on your sweet corn crop.

A word of warning: you must get the corn off to a good start before planting the squash or the squash can smother it while it's still short. Planting out the corn two weeks before the squash is recommended. Another word of warning: beware of the famous Native American combination of maize, squash and climbing beans, in which the bean uses the maize stalk as a climbing frame. It works in the southwest of

Ruby chard and broad beans.

North America, but I've never heard of it working in the UK. Polyculture combinations can be quite specific to local conditions.

Another combination of a tall narrow plant with a short bushy one is leeks and celeriac. An advantage of this combination is that both are planted out and harvested at the same time of year, so there is never a time when the bed is only half used by the combined crop.

Sharing Time

Garlic and summer lettuce is another tall-short mix. These two plants have a different annual cycle, but in this case that works to your advantage. The garlic is planted at normal spacing in autumn and, in late spring or early summer, lettuce seedlings are planted out between the garlic plants. They use the horizontal space between the garlic plants, then the garlic is harvested and they have the remaining space to grow into. Thus we make the maximum use of the resources of space and time.

Lettuce and cabbage is another combination that does the same thing. Both are planted out together and the quicker-growing lettuce is harvested before the cabbages have expanded to use all the space available for them. All the slower growing brassicas can be intercropped in this way. There may even be time to get a crop of early leeks between purple sprouting broccoli before they take up all the space they finally need, though I don't know of anyone who's tried this.

Brussels sprouts and summer cabbage have been mixed in this way at Wellesbourne Research Station, yielding up to a third more overall than both crops in monoculture would yield on the same area. Putting two brassicas together does lose the plant health advantages of a polyculture. But it can be simpler having all the brassicas together, for example in rotation planning or if you need to net them against pests.

An old favourite that works with time is parsnips and radish. Sow them both in the same row and you'll be pulling the radishes long before the parsnips are big enough for the two to compete. This has an added advantage. Parsnips are so slow to germinate that you often need to hoe the bed for weeds before the parsnips come up, but don't dare because you can't see where the parsnips are. The radishes will be well up by then and act as a marker for the parsnip rows.

I know someone who tried a three-way mix of radish, carrot and parsnip, hoping to harvest each one in turn before it started competing with the next slower growing one. But it turned out there wasn't enough difference between the growth patterns of the carrots and the parsnips. Maybe it would work with a very short season carrot variety.

Helping Hands

All the above combinations are based on avoiding competition by combining plants that differ in their use of space and time. But some crops can actually help each other.

One combination that is often quoted is carrots and onions. The scent of the onions is meant to smother that of the carrots and thus confuse the carrot root flies. It works, but only if you plant four rows of onion to every one of carrots. This is fine if you want carrots and onions in these proportions, but if you eat as many carrots as onions it's not much use.

Yucca, fig and gage.

Another combination that is better in theory than in practice is mixing legume crops – peas and beans – with leafy crops, so that the latter can benefit from the nitrogen fixed by the legumes. The leafy vegetables are only going to get any of this nitrogen when both crops have grown enough so that their roots are intermixed. With annual plants this is not likely to happen until fairly well on into the season, and any benefits are doubtful.

Planting the two very close together would increase competition, and this would probably outweigh any advantage. In fact it's hard to think of a combination of legume and non-legume where the growth habit is as different as it is in the tall-short examples given above. Without this kind of difference there is always the likelihood that competition will outweigh resource sharing.

A possible exception is runner beans. When grown in a double row or a tipi, lettuce and other salad crops can be grown between the rows or beneath the tipi before the beans grow enough to cut out too much light. But the benefit to the salad plants is not so much from the nitrogen as from the shade and shelter that the beans give. In hot summer weather, salad plants and other leafy crops like spinach actually benefit from a bit of shade.

Sweet corn can also provide this kind of partial shade to salad crops, and here the season is longer because they never cast too much. In fact you could say that it's a waste of space not to under-plant sweet corn. Delicious as it is, it gives a low yield per square metre and uses the space rather poorly.

Squash growing beneath corn.

Marigolds with celeriac.

Tomatoes with Japanese wineberry..

Sweet corn under planted with beetroot.

Plants can also help each other by giving shelter from wind. Alternate beds of tall crops and tender ones can be effective. But make sure the beds or rows are aligned at right angles to the prevailing wind. If they run parallel to it they will act as a wind tunnel and actually increase the wind. Peas and beans can give shelter to outdoor tomatoes in this way.

Where there's enough space, fruit can be brought into the picture. In the Fens of East Anglia, bulbs have been grown between wire-trained blackberries. Espalier and fan trained tree fruits can be used in the same way, though they should never be expected to fulfil the function of windbreaks on a really windy site. Rows should always run north to south to prevent excessive shading. If they run east to west, one side will be in shade all day. Alternatively the fruit can be planted round the vegetables in a horseshoe to create a suntrap.

Take it from Here

In all these combinations you're planting more plants per square metre than you would with monocultures. You're covering the ground more completely and more quickly, so weeds get less of a look-in, which means less work.

This begs the question of just how to space the plants. Can they all go in at normal spacing, thus doubling up the total number of plants, or should they be a little more widely spaced, giving a plant density of say 130 or 150% of normal?

With some – garlic and lettuce, cabbage and lettuce, sweet corn and salads – you can certainly go for normal spacing. With others – leeks and celeriac, Brussels sprouts and cabbage – you should probably aim for something like 130% of normal plant density. But these are only rough guidelines and note that I won't stick my neck out on sweet corn and squash. A lot depends on your local climate, the season, the fertility of your garden, how good a gardener you are, and above all, what feels right to you.

These are just a few simple combinations, and none of them are for more than two plants together. I'm pretty confident they will work in most gardens in most seasons. But regard them as a starting point. Once you get the hang of it you can experiment with more complex polycultures. The key is to observe carefully how different crops grow in your garden. Then ask yourself just how they could be put together so that they co-operate more than they compete with each other. Have fun!

A mix of salad leaves, including mizuna and spinach.

13

Winter Salads

I n the winter months the two absolute stalwarts in my garden are land cress and lamb's lettuce, aka corn salad. They're both salad plants that give their best from autumn to spring. Through the colder months they make up for all the tender plants that are only available in warmer times. Lamb's lettuce gives a mild taste and land cress a slightly more piquant one, a bit like watercress.

As summer comes on they both soon flower and go to seed. The leaves become too small to harvest easily and the taste isn't so good. But if you leave a few plants of each kind in the ground and allow them to complete their annual cycle they'll self seed and provide you with plants for the next winter.

Sometimes they come up so thickly that they make an effective green manure. A green manure is a crop you grow not so much to eat as to benefit the soil. They cover the soil surface and protect it from the elements, while taking up mineral nutrients that would otherwise be leached out of the soil by the winter rain. Keeping the soil occupied by plants throughout the year is also said to benefit mycorrhizal fungi, the fungi that make mutually beneficial relationships with green plants and improve their growth and health. These are just some of the reasons why keeping the soil covered, preferably with living plants, is one of the principles of permaculture.

Because they're mainly active in the winter, lamb's lettuce and land cress can make a good polyculture in combination with plants that leaf in the summer. In my garden, lamb's lettuce often comes up thickly under the raspberry canes making use of the winter sunshine while the raspberries are leafless. This is what we call stacking in permaculture: growing two crops together, one tall and one short, so as to make twice as much use of the ground. It only works because they're active at different times of the year.

Rocket is another plant with a similar annual cycle, though in my garden it only self seeds in the greenhouse. It will do fine if I sow it outside though, and I often do this. Late July is a good time to sow all three plants, though August isn't too late. Much depends on the weather. You can hand sow them each year, of course, but self-seeding saves you some work and I rather like the unpredictability of it. You never quite know when they'll come up, or whereabouts in the garden. One thing you can be sure of though – at least with my two stalwarts – is that they will come up. Once you've sown them you should never need to do so again.

Patrick picking apples.

14

Fruit Trees and Shrubs

When we think of growing some of our own food we usually think first of vegetables, but the best place to start for many of us may be with fruit. Being perennials, fruit trees and shrubs take much less work than a plot of annual vegetables, so they are a good choice for people with busy lives who have little time to spare for gardening. On the whole they are even more delicious than fresh vegetables, especially for children. Picking juicy raspberries and popping them straight in their mouths is an excellent way for them to learn first hand where food comes from. Organic fruit is particularly expensive to buy in the shops, because it's so difficult to grow on a commercial scale. It's much easier in a home garden, where a small amount of fruit is surrounded by other kinds of plants, so pests and diseases are less likely to build up to problem proportions.

One key to success with fruit is choosing the best kinds to grow. The best fruits for any particular garden are likely to be ones that:

▷ Suit the climate of the garden
▷ Suit the soil
▷ Are easy to grow
▷ Can be eaten over a long season
▷ Fit the size of the garden
▷ Are especially liked by the family.

Climate

Most fruits like a warm summer without too much rain. In Britain, the further north or west you are, and the higher you are above sea level, the more restricted your choice of fruit is. For most of the country the rule of thumb is that fruit does best below 120m (395ft) above sea level, but most kinds can be grown up to 180m (590ft) or even higher in particularly favourable spots.

As a rough guide, the following list places the most commonly grown fruits in order of climatic tolerance, starting with the toughest:

Peaches ripe for picking in a greenhouse.

- ▷ Wildings, e.g. bramble, rowan, wild crab
- ▷ Soft fruit
- ▷ Cooking apples, damsons
- ▷ Eating apples, cooking plums
- ▷ Pears, eating plums
- ▷ Gages, tender pears
- ▷ Peaches, apricots, figs etc.

There is also a great range of toughness among the different varieties of these fruits. Much can be learned from nursery catalogues, particularly those that specialise in varieties suitable for their own part of the country.

A good guide to what will do well in your garden is to see what is successful in similar gardens in the same locality. Neighbouring gardens may have quite different climatic conditions from one another, or a different microclimate, as the specific climate of a small area is called. So it's important to compare like with like. Three conditions that are important for fruit and can vary over very short distances are frost, wind and shade. A late spring frost can kill fruit blossom, which means no fruit that year. It can happen anywhere, but it's much more likely in what's known as a frost pocket. These are places where frost can strike when the rest of the landscape is free of it. Because cold air sinks, they are often found in a hollow in the landscape, or a place where the downward flow of cold air is dammed up by a wall or thick hedge. If at all possible, frost pockets are best avoided for fruit, but blackberries and hybrid berries have a little frost tolerance, and late-flowering varieties of other fruits may miss spring frosts.

Wind can destroy blossom too, and damage the fruit itself later in the year. Tree fruits are much more vulnerable to wind than soft fruits, and the latter are the best choice for a windy garden, unless it's possible to grow a windbreak.

As for shade, there are two rules of thumb:

▷ Tree fruits need more sunlight than soft fruits.
▷ Eaters need more sunlight than cookers.

Most soft fruits and cookers can manage with half a day's full sunlight, while eating varieties of tree fruits are best grown in full sun.

Most gardens have a variety of microclimates within them, and fruit will be much more successful if the different kinds are placed in the position they like best. For example, most pears need a sheltered and sunny position, red and white currants can do well by a north-facing wall, and a tough damson can actually be used as a windbreak plant.

Soil

There are two soil conditions which most fruits really dislike: poor drainage and a thin soil over chalk.

If the drainage is less than perfect, the best choices among the commonly grown fruits are: cooking apples, crab apples, blackcurrants and blackberries. If it's really bad you will need to do something about improving it before you can grow fruit.

Apricots, figs and blackberries can do well on a thin chalk soil. If there's a good spade's depth of soil above the chalk, most fruits, except raspberries and blueberries, will be alright.

The elder is a lesser-grown fruit that can tolerate either imperfect drainage or a chalky soil.

Ease of Growing

By and large the tougher fruits are the easiest to grow, and the ranking for climate tolerance (see 'Climate' page 103) is also a rough guide to ease of growing.

For organic growing, resistance to disease is particularly important. Crab apples, figs, kiwis and elders are generally untroubled by disease, but among the more commonly grown fruits it's more a matter of choosing resistant varieties.

Apples are most troubled by scab and canker in high rainfall areas and by mildew in drier areas, and resistant varieties are available to suit both situations. It's also wise to choose pears that are resistant to scab and fireblight, and gooseberries that are resistant to mildew. Virus diseases can affect all varieties of soft fruit equally, but certain varieties are available as certified virus-free planting stock, and it's as well to use these unless there's a compelling reason to choose another variety.

Desert King fig.

Early Transparent gage.

Length of Season

There are three ways of lengthening the season over which you can enjoy your home-grown fruit:

- ▷ Growing a range of fruits and varieties.
- ▷ Growing fruits and varieties that keep for a long time.
- ▷ Bottling, making jam and freezing.

Unless you're blessed with a large garden, it's much easier to grow a range of different soft fruits than tree fruits, simply because the plants are much smaller. By and large the soft fruits are ready in the earlier part of the season, the summer, and the tree fruits later, in the autumn.

The only fruits that really keep without being preserved in some way are apples and pears. Pears don't keep for very long, though there is a difference between varieties, and pride of place for keeping goes to apples. There's a whole range of varieties, from the very earliest that hardly keep at all to the latest that can keep until spring if you store them carefully. If you only have space for one tree, it's best to make it a keeping apple, which you can enjoy over a period of several months.

With non-keeping tree fruits, such as plums and early season apples and pears, even a single tree can easily produce more than the family can eat fresh. The surplus

Brown Turkey fig developing.

Apple and pear harvest.

can be given away, bartered or sold, or it can be preserved in one way or another. When planning a fruit garden it's all too easy to get carried away and think that once the fruit is there you will get into bottling and jam-making. You may well do, but don't count on it: it's a lot of work, and has to be done when the fruit is ready, not when you feel like it.

Pollination

This is an added consideration when choosing varieties of tree fruits. Most of the commonly grown tree fruits need pollen from another tree to fertilise them in order to set fruit. This tree must be of the same species but a different variety. There are exceptions: a few pears are partially self-fertile (will give some crop without a pollinator), while quite a number of plums and most damsons are fully self-fertile.

If there are plenty of apple trees in neighbouring gardens you may be able to grow a single apple with some confidence that it will be pollinated, but in most cases it's safer to grow two or more trees which can pollinate each other.

The trees must flower at the same time. Apples, pears and plums are divided into pollination groups, each group consisting of varieties that flower together. Trees that are in the same group, or the one immediately before or after it, can pollinate each other successfully. Nursery catalogues give the pollination group of all the varieties they offer.

Size of Garden

In a small garden it's clearly easier to find space for soft fruit than for trees, but there are ways of making the trees smaller.

The first is growing them on dwarf rootstocks. Any fruiting variety can be grafted onto a range of rootstocks that restrict the size of the tree to varying degrees. There is a much wider range for apples than there is for other fruits, down to the 'extremely dwarfing' that gives a tree of less than two metres diameter. Pears and plums will always be bigger than this even on the smallest rootstock, the actual size depending on the variety.

The second is to grow trees in restricted forms. These are the two-dimensional espalier, fan or cordon shapes, which are trained on a fence or up against a wall. These take up very little space, and though the yield per tree is not very high the yield per square metre is more than you can get from open-grown trees.

Even where space is not a limitation, growing smaller trees means you can grow a wider range of varieties, and avoid overproduction of any one kind. The downside is that both dwarf and restricted form trees require much more care and attention than large or medium-sized open-grown trees.

For very small gardens the hybrid berries are a good choice. They can be grown up walls and fences, leaving as much of the horizontal space as possible for other uses. Some hybrids need more space per plant than others, and a good nursery catalogue will indicate the space needed for each kind.

What You Like

This is often the one consideration that has to be balanced against all the others put together. Obviously there's no point in growing something that isn't going to be eaten, and you may push at some of the constraints of climate, soil and size to include a real favourite.

Beware of curiosities. These include apple varieties with interesting names, and less useful fruits like medlars and quinces. I would recommend only growing fruits that you have tasted and know you like.

This applies more to tree fruits than soft fruits. On the whole there is more difference between the taste of different tree fruit varieties, especially apples, and a tree is a big investment in both space and time. It will be at least a couple of years before you eat the fruit of a tree you plant. If you then find you don't like it, will you grub it out and start again, or will you religiously munch fruit you don't really like for the rest of your life?

Planting to Harvest Time Lag

Some people are put off growing fruit because of the time lag between planting and enjoying the full harvest. But you can be eating soft fruit in the year after planting it, and most of the trees that are suitable for gardens will start to bear fruit after 3-5 years. These days many of us move house rather often, and we may be reluctant to invest in something we're not going to reap the full benefit of. Personally I don't mind if someone else gets the benefit of my work. I like the old saying, "Live as though you're going to die tomorrow, but farm as though you're going to live forever." Much the same goes for gardening.

Our Own Selection

As an example, here is the selection of fruit my partner and I grow. Our rented house has a medium-sized garden, and we also have a field a few miles away where we grow a range of tree fruits. When we moved in, the following fruits were already in the garden:
▷ Pear, Williams. Not a good choice for this rather windy site, and they are dependent on neighbours' trees for pollination, but we get a good crop in some years.
▷ Gooseberries and red currants. We don't like them much, and have removed them.
▷ Cultivated blackberries. We've kept these.

We've planted these in the garden:
▷ Raspberries. Two summer fruiting varieties, early and late (we're usually working away from home during the autumn fruiting raspberry season).
▷ Veitchberry. A form of loganberry (a cross between raspberry and blackberry), which fills the gap between the summer raspberries and the blackberries.
▷ All the garden fruit is grown round the edge of the garden, leaving plenty of open space in the middle for perennial vegetables.

Homemade peach jam.

Away from Home

In our field (a few miles from our house), we've planted a small orchard consisting of two walnuts, four cobnuts, five apples and three pears. We decided against plums because of the distance from home – you have to be around to catch them when they're ripe.

As an example of choosing varieties, these are the apples we went for:

Red currants.

Charles Ross apple.

Bardsey Island apple.

▷ Worcester Pearmain. September-October. The most delicious early apple; a close neighbour has a very productive one, grown organically.

▷ Charles Ross. October-November. Keeps well for an early variety and tastes quite good; grown locally, scab resistant, does well on chalky soil. (Although there is a good depth of topsoil in the field, there is lime underneath it, and this variety is included as a bit of insurance as much as anything.)

▷ Egremont Russet. October-December. A rare and delicate flavour; very disease resistant and recommended for organic growing.

▷ Kidd's Orange Red. November-January. The most delicious apple on Earth, and beautiful to look at; grown commercially in the locality, resistant to scab, but susceptible to canker – a bit of a risk.

▷ Pixie. December-March. The only one we haven't tasted, but we wanted a good late fan keeper and didn't know one personally; resistant to scab.

All the apples are in pollination groups 2, 3 and 4, 0.

Merton Pride pear.

Currant bush in flower.

An espalier rootstock is an alternative to dwarf rootstocks.

15

Planting Fruit Trees

Which Fruit?

If you want to have a varied selection of fruit trees to choose from, you shouldn't wait until planting time in the winter to buy your trees. To be sure you get the trees that really meet your needs, it's advisable to get your order in by August. Beyond that you may well find that the tree or trees you want are sold out. And it's worthwhile choosing your trees with care. They will last many decades, maybe your whole lifetime or more. If you find your trees yield fruit your family doesn't like, or too much of it all at one time, or that they grow too big for the space available for them, you will have plenty of time to regret not having taken more care over your choice.

Apples to Peaches

Have you ever wondered why the apple is far and away the most common fruit grown in Britain? The main reason is that it grows so well here. It's reliable. To some extent there's a trade-off between reliability and deliciousness of the fruit, with a range that runs something like this:
 ▷ Cooking apples, dessert apples, pears
 ▷ Damsons, plums, gages, peaches and apricots.

Some others need special conditions: figs need an almost frost-free microclimate, while cherries will yield nothing if not protected from birds, unless you grow a whole orchard of them, that is.

If you live in a cool, rainy area or your garden is shady, cooking apples and damsons are most likely to yield well. But don't think of growing peaches and apricots unless you have a favourable microclimate, and preferably a nice south-facing wall onto which you can fan train them and give them all the care and attention they need. Here in Britain they're far to the north of their natural range.

Food or Experiment?

Many permaculturists are fired by an enthusiasm for unusual plants, including fruit. Books such as Ken Fern's, *Plants for a Future*, are full of inspiring descriptions of unfamiliar species that could be grown here. But beware. If a plant isn't commonly grown it may be for a good reason. It may not taste that good or it may not yield well in our climate.

A microclimate in Hampshire, England, where fig and yucca grow.

I don't want to discourage anyone from experimenting with new fruits, but before you devote valuable space to a tree that will live for decades, be clear about your main aim. Is it to put food on your table or to experiment? If it's the former, you would be well advised to stick with apples, pears and plums.

Keeping/Storing

Plums and other stone fruits don't keep. You either have to eat them quickly or preserve them by bottling, freezing or some other method. This requires work and it's easy to overestimate the amount of enthusiasm you'll have for preserving when the tree grows to maturity and produces more than you and your family can eat fresh.

Peach growing in the greenhouse, alongside tomatoes, chillies and hanging strawberries.

Pears keep a bit longer but pride of place goes to apples. I keep apples in my garden shed simply by putting them in used boxes and trays which I scrump from the local market, and we eat fresh apples from September right through to the following May. To do that you need a good mix of apple varieties.

Which Variety?

There's a bewildering range of varieties available. It may seem best just to go for something you've heard of, like Cox apple and Victoria plum, or just accept the meagre offering of the local garden centre. But these trees will last you a lifetime. Why not get the ones that will suit you and your garden perfectly. All you need is a good mail-order nursery catalogue and/or a good book.

Taste

Plant what you and your family like to eat. Written descriptions are a help but there's really no substitute for tasting them before choosing. Beware of shop-bought fruit. It will have been picked unripe and ripened off the tree and some varieties will never reach their full flavour like this. Try to find neighbours with trees of the varieties you're interested in.

Pollination

Most fruit trees can't set fruit without being pollinated by another tree of the same species but a different variety. If you live in a village or an old suburb there will probably be enough fruit trees in other people's gardens to provide pollination partners. But in a more isolated situation you have to plant two apple trees in order to get any apples.

There's some difference between the different fruits:
▷ All apple trees need a pollinating partner.
▷ Almost all varieties of pear do too.
▷ About half the plum varieties do and the other half are 'self-fertile', so you can grow just one if you choose the right variety.

You also need to make sure that your pollinating partners flower at the same time. The nursery catalogue will assign each variety to a pollination group, according to their relative flowering time. Varieties in the same group or an adjacent group will pollinate each other. Thus a tree in group 2 will pollinate one in group 1, 2 or 3 but not one in group 4.

Disease Resistance

It's a good idea to choose varieties that have natural disease resistance, especially if you live towards the wetter west of the country or at high altitude, where fruit growing is marginal. In apples and pears, scab and canker are the most important diseases to watch out for in wetter regions, and mildew in drier ones.

Spreading the Harvest

Above I praised the apple as the fruit that keeps over the longest eating season – late August to May – without any precautions other than placing them carefully in a garden shed. But to do that you need a mix of varieties. They divide up into:

▷ **Earlies:** mostly ripen in September, only keep for a month

▷ **Mid-season:** harvest in October, ripe immediately or around Christmas, usually have a two month eating season

▷ **Late keepers:** harvest in October, start eating in January and some varieties keep right through till May.

Notice how the later ripening ones keep the longest. So, if you're planting a lot of trees I recommend that you plant them in the ratio, 1 early: 2 mid-season: 4 late keepers. This will give you a constant supply. And if you only have space for one tree, make it a late-keeping apple.

Pinova apple on a M27 dwarf rootstock. Grown as a step-over to save space..

Heritage Varieties

If preserving ancient, local varieties is one of your aims in growing fruit, I wouldn't want to discourage you. But if your main aim is to feed your family, heritage varieties may not be best. 'Heritage' means that most people don't grow them any more and there's probably a good reason for it. Often it's taste or disease resistance. Modern varieties have been carefully selected for both these qualities by generations of plant breeders.

On the other hand, a variety that does well in your area is likely to do well for you. If you can, find out what other fruit growers locally are growing, and then taste the fruit. Also, don't be afraid to break the rules. Kidd's Orange Red is, in my opinion, the best tasting apple in the world but it's also very susceptible to canker. Nonetheless I couldn't resist planting one myself and, though it has got canker, year after year it has yielded abundant harvests of the most delicious fruit.

Which Rootstock?

Almost all fruit trees are grafted onto a rootstock. This means that the tree is actually two genetically distinct individuals, united by the skilful hand of the grafter. One of these is the rootstock, comprising the roots and the lower portion of the trunk, while the other, known as the scion, is all the rest of the plant: most of the trunk, branches, leaves and fruit. The scion is the fruiting variety, e.g. Cox, Bramley etc. and determines what the fruit is like. Meanwhile the rootstock determines certain characteristics of the tree as a whole:

▷ **Size**. Rootstocks are classified as vigorous, i.e. full size, or dwarf, with various intermediates such as 'semi-dwarfing' and so on. (The variety also affects the size of the tree, but to a lesser extent.)

▷ **Vigour.** Dwarf trees are like infants throughout their lives. Vigorous trees only need to be staked and weeded or mulched for their first 3-4 years and then can look after themselves, but dwarfs need this level of care forever.

▷ **Life cycle.** Dwarf trees start bearing fruit a year or two after planting and have a short overall life, as little as 25 years for extremely dwarfing rootstocks. Vigorous trees may not start bearing for 8-10 years but can have a productive life of a century or more.

How to Choose Rootstocks

One aim of permaculture is to keep the need for maintenance low, so it might seem that vigorous trees would be the thing. But there are some disadvantages to these big trees:

▷ **Yield.** A single vigorous tree can produce over 100kg of fruit per year. Can your family eat that much, especially if it's a non-keeping kind such as a stone fruit or an early season apple? It may be better to have two or three smaller trees of different varieties.

▷ **Space.** The most vigorous pears can have a diameter of 20m and apples easily 10m, and you may need two of each for pollination.

▷ **Reach.** Vigorous trees are tall and all picking, pruning etc. needs to be done from a ladder. A dwarf is reachable from the ground or a little step up.

▷ **Life cycle.** Most of us want to start harvesting some fruit within a couple of years of planting.

So the advantages of vigour and dwarfness need to be balanced and there are plenty of good stocks that fall in the middle of the size range that combine the advantages of both.

If you want to grow your tree or trees in a restricted form, i.e. the two-dimensional espalier or fan shapes that make such good use of the favourable microclimate up against a wall, you will need to use a relatively vigorous stock. The intensive pruning that goes with this style of growing reduces their vigour anyway. The same goes for fruit trees in pots or other containers: the pot will reduce the size of the root system, so a more vigorous stock is needed to balance this out.

If your soil is poor or your climate challenging, the standard advice is to use a more vigorous rootstock than you would if conditions were more favourable.

A mix of Patrick's apple harvest.

Some Suggestions:

▷ **Apples**. M26 is a good stock for medium to large gardens. It makes a tree of 2.5-4m diameter, depending on variety and soil conditions. It's the smallest apple stock that doesn't need staking and mulching throughout its life. MM106 is ideal for orchards. Diameter is 4-6m and you should get your first fruit within two years of planting.

▷ **Pears**. Quince A is the best all-round stock, giving a tree between 3-7m diameter. If you're short of space you might try the smaller Quince C but only if you can provide the best soil conditions and good care.

▷ **Plums**. St Julien A, at about 3m diameter is the usual choice, with Pixy a slightly smaller alternative.

▷ **Cherries**. The problem with cherries is that if you only have one or two trees, the birds will eat all the fruit, so you have to net them. It's much easier to net a short tree than a tall one and the dwarfing stock for cherries is Gisela.

Pruning keeps a tree healthy creating air circulation and preventing branches from rubbing which can cause disease.

16

Pruning

Pruning is an important aspect of maintenance in the garden. It reduces the risk of disease and creates a healthy environment for plants to grow in.

Pruning Apples

My friend Colum and I share crop the apples. I grew the trees and they're on land which used to be mine but which I've since donated to the Somerset Wildlife Trust. I still keep the little orchard which I grew in one corner of the field. Colum and I share the work equally and share the crop one-third/two-thirds.

But you can't call it work. A trip together into the deep country for half a day to be in a landscape we love, doing things we love doing. It's probably as much or more fun than other men get from going to a football match. I say 'or more' because we just have three fixtures a year, so they have scarcity value.

In September we pick the early apples, Worcester Pearmain. It's the second most delicious apple on Earth, with a light, aromatic flavour if ripened on the tree. These always provide the fruit for our September permaculture design course. Charles Ross are a reliable dual purpose fruit and some years they're ready in September too, others not till later.

In October we pick the maincrop: Egremont Russet, Kidd's Orange Red and Pixie. Pixie's a great little keeping apple. They'll keep till May with no problem. Kidd's Orange Red is not only the most delicious apple on Earth, it's also the most beautiful.

This year the leaves are off the trees earlier than they have been for many years. Usually we prune in December but this year it was the last day in November.

That makes three visits within three months. The rest of the year we hardly touch the trees. Perhaps a tad of summer pruning if I remember it, some fruit thinning, though never as much as I should. All the real activity is concentrated in one part of the year. From a work point of view apples don't so much have an annual cycle as a season, Apple Autumn.

Patrick and Colum's top tips for pruning an established tree:
▷ Get the best pruning tools you can and keep them sharp.
▷ Make clean cuts, at an angle which sheds the rain.
▷ First take out the 3 Ds – anything that's dead, diseased or damaged
▷ Then branches which are crossing – they can rub and damage each other.

- ▷ Then branches which grow towards the middle of the tree.
- ▷ Lastly, any which are too crowded – fruiting branches should ideally be 22cm (9in) apart.
- ▷ If in doubt, leave it.

Pruning Raspberries

This is another winter job. The first thing to do is to determine whether your raspberries are summer fruiting or autumn fruiting. If your canes give fruit in June or July, they are summer fruiting. September or later and they're autumn fruiting.

Pruning autumn fruiting varieties is simple: you just cut down all the canes. They give fruit on canes which are in their first year of growth, after which there is no reason to keep them.

Summer fruiting ones are only slightly less simple. They give fruit on canes, which are in their second year of growth. So every winter you need to cut out all the second year canes, which have already fruited, and leave all the first year ones, which are still to fruit. Telling the difference between the two is easy once you've got your eye in: second year canes are branched and first year canes are not. There's often a colour difference too, the second year ones being paler than the first year's, but not always. The branching is the clear difference you can always rely on.

When you've taken out all the second year canes, have a look round and take out any very small ones, which are obviously going to come to nothing. Likewise any canes which are crossing each other, where they will rub each other and let in pest and diseases. If the remaining canes are very dense, thin them out till the average distance between them is 22cm (9in). I find I very rarely need to do that.

Decide how tall you want the canes to be and cut off any that are taller than that. Personally I trim down to about chest height, 1.2m (4ft). Usually only one or two need shortening. Always cut back to just above a bud.

Raspberries spread by suckering. That is, new canes come up from the roots. As the roots spread, some of them will come up outside your designated raspberry bed. You may want to dig out the suckers if they're invading a productive vegetable bed or other valued area. But every few years it's a good idea to let them have their head and move to new ground. This helps to keep them free, or at least tolerant, of virus diseases, and if you let them wander slowly round the garden you can get away without buying new stock every dozen years. As they advance on one side you can dig them up where they've been for longest and follow them with vegetables or other fruits. Don't follow them with other cane fruits though, as they share the same soil-borne diseases.

A dwarf apple pruned to grow as a step-over – great for small gardens.

Raspberry canes grown and trained in rows.

 1. Observe & interact

 2. Catch & store energy

 3. Obtain a yield

 4. Apply self-regulation & accept feedback

 5. Use & value renewable resources & services

 6. Produce no waste

 7. Design from patterns to details

 8. Integrate rather than segregate

 9. Use small & slow solutions

 10. Use & value diversity

 11. Use edges & value the marginal

12. Creatively use & respond to change

17

Permaculture Principles Beyond the Garden

The basic idea of permaculture is that we take natural ecosystems as the model for what we do ourselves. This is all very well if you have a farm or woodland to work with, or even a large garden. But what about people who only have a small urban garden, or even no garden at all? How can they use permaculture?

It would be pretty difficult if permaculture was always a direct imitation of an ecosystem, like a forest garden for example. But it doesn't have to be. The essence of permaculture is not in copying the outward appearance of natural systems but in understanding the principles by which they work and applying these to our activities (see image opposite).

One of the things which makes an ecosystem work is the network of useful links between all its components. An example is the relationship between flowering plants and pollinating insects, where one gets its reproductive needs met and the other gets fed. There are many similar links we can make in our own lives, and these can reduce the ecological impact of getting our needs met.

Another thing we can learn from ecology is that in a mature ecosystem the most successful plants and animals are those that minimise their need for energy and other inputs. Pioneer plants use up masses of energy producing tens of thousands of seeds per plant, but their day is soon past. They're soon superseded by plants which produce much less but which persist indefinitely. The lesson for us is plain.

Ecological Impact

If the aim of permaculture is to reduce our harmful ecological impact, the first step must be to look at which aspects of our lives have the biggest impact. The book, *Our Ecological Footprint*, comes up with the proportions shown in a pie chart.

Other studies have come up with different proportions to these, some with transport rather than food taking the biggest slice. It all depends on what weightings you give to different kinds of impact – how much global warming equals the loss of one species? – and how you allocate things. If you include flying green beans in from Kenya under transport, then food will get off very lightly.

I've even heard it said that if a person stops driving to work and walks instead their ecological impact can go up, because the ecological cost of the extra food they eat due to the exercise is greater than that of driving! I don't mean to suggest we should all drive to work, but that eating locally-grown organic food is perhaps the most important thing we can do to help the planet.

Food

Permaculture places a great deal of emphasis on food. This is partly because it was first conceived of as an alternative to agriculture and only later expanded to include other aspects of life. But the dominance of food in the *Ecological Footprint* study suggests that this emphasis is wholly appropriate.

Only one per cent of our energy consumption is used in farming, but twelve times as much is used in transporting, processing, packaging and marketing it.

Energy use is only a rough indicator of ecological impact. Since farms cover much of the land surface of the world they have a greater direct impact on biodiversity, for example, than many other human activities. Nevertheless the energy ratio suggests that where we get our food from is at least as important as how it's grown.

Would you rather eat an organic apple air-freighted from New Zealand or one from five miles away which has been sprayed with 24 doses of pesticide in its short life?

Importing dry foods, such as grain, nuts and pulses, has much less impact. Because they're not perishable they're transported by sea or land rather than air. The transport cost per calorie is much less in any case because they contain very little water, compared to 90% water in fruit and vegetables.

Of course the ideal is to eat food which is both local and organic. But 70% of the organic produce eaten in Britain is imported. So a third priority is to encourage more British farmers and growers to go organic, so that more of us can eat truly wholesome food without incurring the ecological costs of long-distance transport.

We can use the permaculture principle of making links to achieve all three aims. The link here is a direct one between producer and consumer. By joining a Box Scheme, where fruit and vegetables are sold directly to the consumers by the growers, we not only know exactly where the food came from and how it was grown, we also make organic growing more financially viable to the producers and thus encourage more local organic production.

On average only 10p in every pound spent in a supermarket goes to the person who actually grew the food. But when we buy direct it all goes to them. Even allowing for the extra work and expense of operating the Box Scheme, the growers make a far better living than they could by selling to a supermarket. This especially applies to small growers, who don't have the economies of scale on their side.

An even more powerful link can be made by joining a subscription farming scheme, or Community Supported Agriculture (CSA) as it's sometimes known. In these schemes you don't pay for your produce by the week; you buy a share at the beginning of the season and take a share in the harvest. Payment by instalments is usually available to people who can't find all the money at once. But the more people can pay up front the better, as it keeps the farmers out of debt, and interest payments can swallow up most of their income if they have to borrow to finance the sowing of the crop.

Farmers' Markets are another direct link between producers and consumers. Most of them stipulate that the food must be grown within a certain radius of the market and that the person on the stall must be the farmer or someone who works on the farm. The produce doesn't have to be organic, but these markets provide an ideal opportunity to talk to the producers face to face and perhaps persuade them to go organic.

Any food we grow for ourselves will have even less ecological impact than what we buy from local sources. Even people without gardens can grow some of their own food by sprouting seeds. Sprouting turns a relatively indigestible food with a negligible vitamin content into little plants which are highly digestible and have a higher vitamin content than at any other time in their lives. This increase in food value is definitely a form of food production rather than preparation, and anyone can have a mini-garden in their kitchen.

Transport

Trains are not ecologically friendly; they're just less damaging than cars. The first choice to make in transport is not between the lesser of two evils but to live in a place where we don't need to make long trips to work, school, shops and so on. For most of us this means living in the town. The idea that the permacultural ideal is to live in the country is only true for the minority of us who actually make our living there, and want to live a simple lifestyle.

This is the principle of linking again. Links can only happen when we place things appropriately, and this is why permaculture is often seen as a design system. Design starts with our whole lifestyles, and we need to place ourselves where we can make the journeys we need to without using fossil fuels.

Becoming car-free is the biggest single change most of us can make to green our lifestyles, but not all of us are willing or able to take that step. A good intermediate step is to join a car sharing club. These are already well-developed in many Continental countries and are just starting up in Britain.

The beauty of car sharing is that it reverses the financial incentive to use a car for every little trip. When you own your own, most of the costs are fixed costs and the cost of a single extra journey is only a little petrol. In a car share club you pay a proportion of the whole cost for each trip, so the less you use a car the more you save of the fixed costs. The result is that people who share typically save £1,000 to £2,000 a year, and masses of carbon dioxide.

Air travel is even more destructive than car. Not only do aeroplanes use more fuel, they deposit the exhaust gasses high in the atmosphere, where, by one estimate, each molecule causes 30 times the damage of one released at ground level. It has been calculated that one round trip to Florida uses up each passenger's entire lifetime allowance of carbon dioxide output, at the level we need to achieve if we're going to stabilise the Earth's climate. Personally I've decided never to fly again – though I wouldn't try to impose that choice on other people.

Housing

Once again, the first decision is where to live. One of the most energy-efficient forms of housing is the terrace house. Each house shares some of its heat with its neighbours, and there's little external surface through which heat can be lost to the outside. Compare this to the other extreme, a detached bungalow, which has a much greater surface area compared to volume.

When it comes to increasing the energy efficiency of a house, simple, cheap things usually give a better return in both cash and energy terms than more high-tech improvements. The latest central heating systems using condensing boilers are amazingly efficient. But if you throw out the old system before it comes to the end of its life you're also discarding some of the energy which went to make it in the first place, the 'embodied energy' as it's known. It's expensive, and you may not even come out ahead in energy terms. Much the same applies to sealed-unit double glazing.

Draught-proofing can give an excellent return in an old house. Putting tin foil behind any radiator on an external wall reflects heat back into the house rather than losing it to the outside by conduction through the wall. Increasing the thickness of insulation in the loft to 300 or even 450mm (12 or 18in), compared to the standard 150mm (6in), is also well worthwhile.

If you do need to replace a worn out appliance, such as a fridge or washing machine, shop around. There are big differences in energy performance between different models, and the most efficient are not necessarily any more expensive.

Having got our energy consumption down from pioneer-plant levels to that appropriate for a successful life in a mature ecosystem, we can start to look at what kind of energy to use. There's no way that renewables can support the present per-capita consumption in our culture. Putting up a windmill in the back garden is not practical for most of us, but there are now a number of electricity companies which supply only renewables, at very little extra cost.

Consumer Goods

Once again, the first question to ask is not which things we buy but how much we buy altogether. There are useful choices to be made between different products. For example, conventional cotton consumes enormous amounts of irrigation water and pesticides in its production, and it is now possible to buy organic cotton products, or even hemp or linen, which could be grown here in Britain. But no sustainable system could support the sheer quantity we consume.

The idea of fashion has much to answer for here. We need to reinvent a culture in which it's perfectly acceptable to be dressed the same way this year as last, or to use the same bathroom ware our grandparents did. One good rule of thumb is to buy things which are made to last. They will probably work out cheaper in the long run. Another is to buy second-hand whenever possible.

Helpful People

Perhaps the most useful links we can make are those with other people who are on the same path. One of the most difficult things about greening our lifestyles is the feeling that we're on our own. Nothing can help more than mutual support between those who share the same aims.

The best way to start is to go on a permaculture course, whether an Introductory weekend or the longer Design Course. These courses enable you to get a deeper understanding of permaculture than can ever be had from reading books and magazine articles. Meeting a lot of like-minded people can be one of the most empowering and enjoyable aspects of a permaculture course.

To help you access like-minded people in your own area, you can join the Permaculture Association and they will provide you with a list of all members in your area. You will probably find that most of them are keen gardeners.

Resources

Where to buy seed

The Organic Gardening Catalogue has a comprehensive range of mainstream seeds and other gardening requisites. They're connected to the charity Garden Organic and buying from them helps to support its valuable work.
www.organiccatalogue.com

The Real Seed Company is run by a couple of gardeners who grow and eat the vegetables whose seed they sell, all heritage, non-hybrid varieties. They must be the only seed company that encourages their customers to save their own seed, with instructions on the packet (seed saving info isn't on the packet but is online). They also campaign against new laws that aim to restrict genetic diversity.
www.realseeds.co.uk

Potatoes are a special case. Blight disease makes it very difficult to grow them successfully without spraying. Even certified organic potatoes are sprayed. But new blight-resistant varieties have been bred by the Sarvari Trust and are available from Thompson and Morgan under the name Sarpo.

Fruit trees

Keepers Nursery: **www.keepers-nursery.co.uk**

Agroforestry Research Trust: **www.agroforestry.co.uk**

Books

Edible Perennial Gardening: Growing Successful Polycultures in Small Spaces by Anni Kelsey. Permanent Publications, 2014.

Forest Gardening in Practice: An Illustrated Practical Guide for Homes, Communities and Enterprises by Tomas Remiarz. Permanent Publications, 2017.

No Dig Organic Home and Garden: Grow, Cook, Use and Store Your Harvest by Charles Dowding and Stephanie Hafferty. Permanent Publications, 2017.

The Earth Care Manual: A Permaculture Handbook For Britain and Other Temperate Climates by Patrick Whitefield. Permanent Publications, 2004.

The Fruit Tree Handbook by Ben Pike. Green Books, 2011.

Photograph Acknowledgements

All photographs copyright to *Permaculture* magazine unless stated below.
All drawings copyright to Patrick Whitefield.

page	
vi	Cathy Whitefield
xii	Minimalist garden – Patrick Whitefield
5	Michael Guerra's garden – Michael Guerra
20	Patrick's minimalist garden – Patrick Whitefield
26	Raised bed – Lynda Watson
28	Two raised beds – Patrick Whitefield
31	Straight raised bed – Patrick Whitefield
32	Easy access bed – Lynda Watson
36	Drystone path – Patrick Whitefield
40	Stone walls – Patrick Whitefield
42-44	Making stone steps, and clapper bridge – Patrick Whitefield
46-52	Cristina's garden – Cristina Crossingham
53-56	Bunkhouse garden – Patrick Whitefield
79	Ramsons – Patrick Whitefield
80	Sea beet – Rmrony/wiki
81	Welsh onion – Patrick Whitefield
	Pink purslane – Roger Griffith/wiki
82	Turkish rocket – Stefan Lefnaer/wiki
	French scorzonera – Paulu/wiki
85	Chickweed – Ivy Main/wiki
	Hairy bittercress – Jay Sturner/wiki
	Fat hen – Harry Rose/wiki
88	Jersey walking kale – Patrick Whitefield
91	Herb patience – Patrick Whitefield
	Musk mallow – Patrick Whitefield
92	Tree onion – Gerwin Sturm/flickr
93	Alpine strawberry – Arvind/wiki
102	Patrick picking apples – Patrick Whitefield
112	Espalier – Patrick Whitefield
119	Apple harvest – Patrick Whitefield
123	Raspberry canes – Trish Steel/geograph
124	Permaculture principles – Holmgren Design Services

Index

References to images are in *italics*.

Books to empower your
head, heart and hands

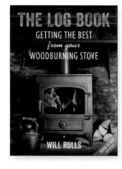

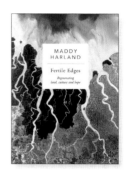

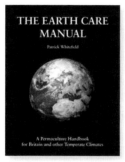

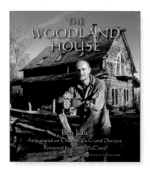

Our titles cover: permaculture, home and garden, green building, food and drink, sustainable technology, woodlands, community, wellbeing and so much more

See Permaculture magazine's full range of books here:

www.permanentpublications.co.uk

Subscribe to a better world

Each issue of Permaculture magazine is hand crafted, sharing practical, innovative solutions, money saving ideas and global perspectives from a grassroots movement in over 170 countries

Print subscribers receive FREE digital access to our complete 25 years of back issues

To subscribe call 01730 823 311 or visit:

www.permaculture.co.uk

See our North American specific edition at: **https://permaculturemag.org**